VOZNESENSKY: *SELECTED POEMS*

Other translations by Herbert Marshall

Mayakovsky

Yevtushenko: Selected Poems

VOZNESENSKY:

Selected Poems

Authorized Translation, with Introduction and Notes,

by HERBERT MARSHALL

REVISED EDITION

 HILL AND WANG · New York

Copyright © 1966 by Herbert Marshall
All rights reserved
ISBN (Clothbound edition) 0–8090–9640–4
ISBN (Paperback edition) 0–8090–1332–0
Library of Congress catalog card number: 66–15896
First edition April 1966

7 8 9 10 11 12

Manufactured in the United States of America

Designed by Bert Clarke

Contents

———————
* Published by Vladimir Knizhnoye Izdatelstvo (Vladimir Book Publishing House) in Vladimir, RSFSR, 1960. Edition of 5,000.
** Published by Sovietsky Pisatel (Publishing House of Soviet Writers), Moscow, 1962. Edition of 50,000.

ANTI-WORLDS*

---

* Published by Molodaya Gvardia (The Young Guard Publishing House),
Moscow, 1964. Edition of 60,000.

---

* Extract from poem "Oza" in *Molodaya Gvardia* ("The Young Guard"), **No.** 10, 1964.
** Published in magazine, *Yunost* ("Youth"), Moscow, 1965.

Translator's Note to the Revised Edition

Owing to circumstances beyond my control, involving a serious illness while abroad, it was not possible for me to check and correct any galley or page proofs of the first (hard cover) editions of New York or London. Hence various errors and mistakes were not corrected and inevitable amendments and improvements not included. I deeply regret this and have awaited the new edition in order that this shall now be done.

I was also unable to express my thanks to Dr. Victor Swoboda and Mr. Batkiw of the School of East European and Slavonic Studies, University of London, for the help they have given me from time to time in this most difficult of all spheres of translation—poetry.

Finally, and as always, my thanks to my wife for everything.

HERBERT MARSHALL

London August 1966

The Poet in Russia

I do not know any country in the world today where so much good poetry is being written or so much poetry is being read or listened to as there is in the Soviet Union. Mother Russia should be proud of her poetic sons and daughters, and yet she seems tragically like Saturn that swallows its own children alive. Each day the battle goes on. But it seems to me that it is now on the side of the poets. Today in the Soviet Union there is definitely a renaissance of poetry, and Andrey Voznesensky is a vital new voice in this renaissance.

"When a poet writes about history," he once said to me, "he doesn't give a damn for the past, he is writing about the present." Although Voznesensky's main concern is a subjective interest in present experience, I would like to explain here the background of a Soviet poet's "present"—and include the past which led to it.

It's difficult for a citizen of a Western European country or of the United States to understand quite how things work in the Soviet Union, particularly in relation to the artist. To begin with, there's only one boss, one power—that is, the Communist Party of the Soviet Union (the CPSU). Theoretically the Soviet Union is a dictatorship of the Proletariat; in practice it is a dictatorship of the Party. And the nature of what it calls "Democratic Centralism" is such that it becomes a dictatorship of the Central Committee and finally of a small caucus, its executive committee, or even of one man in the key position of power, its General Secretary.

So let us be quite clear. An artist in the Soviet Union can only work for this one boss, no matter what name it goes under, whether it be a society, ministry, trade union, limited liability company, cooperative, trust, or any kind of voluntary or cultural organization. In all key matters any Soviet organization whatsoever can be arbitrarily overruled and overridden by the CPSU.

In the early days of the Revolution, when everything was in a state of flux, the power of the Party was not yet consolidated, streamlined, and centralized. There was a degree of liberty allowed to organizations and individuals. In retrospect, it is now seen that this degree of liberty allowed the growth and flowering of the genius of the great Revolutionary artists. Indeed, the greatest artistic works of the Soviet Revolution were produced in this period. The films of Eisenstein and Pudovkin, Dovzhenko, and Vertov, the theatre productions of Meyerhold, Vakhtangov, Tairov, and Mikhoels, the poems of Mayakovsky, Yesenin, Pasternak, and many others. Lenin himself had said: "Everybody is free to write and say what he pleases, without the slightest restrictions, but every free association (and a Party, too) is also free to expel such members who use the Party's platform to preach anti-Party views. Freedom of speech and freedom of the press must be absolute. But the freedom of association must also be absolute."[1] Yet ever since then, official Party spokesmen, including Khrushchev, have been attacking the idea of artistic freedom.

As the degree of liberty disappeared under Stalin, so the quality of Soviet art declined. Today, even after de-Stalinization, the machinery is practically the same. But it is claimed that a return to the "Leninist Norm" is now the policy, and when poets write about the "good old days" of the Lenin period, that is what they have in mind.

In order to earn a living by his art in the Soviet Union, the artist has to join the one organization representing his art, his trade union—for a poet, the Union of Soviet Writers. Until a writer is a member of such an organization, he can get no official commissions for his work. And they are virtually the only commissions. Nor can he get any of the other privileges of the officially recognized Soviet writer, which include publication, state patronage, holiday resorts, writers' homes, and other special advantages.

If for any reason a creative worker is not accepted by the appropriate union, whatever the quality of his work, he will find life very difficult. A recent example was the painter Glazunov. Here is a talented artist, recognized as such both at home and abroad, but he was consistently refused membership in the Union of Soviet Artists, though he paints in the realist tradition. His rejection became so

---

[1] V. I. Lenin, "Party Organization and Party Literature," 1905.

scandalous that the less conservative Union of Soviet Writers made him a member of *their* organization, thus enabling him to have all the privileges refused him by his own union. Eventually the artists' union had to accept him. But when he wanted a Moscow exhibition of his work, the union blocked it, till finally the Ministry of Culture intervened and itself held an exhibition for him in Moscow's Manège Gallery. I was there at the time and saw queues, hundreds of yards long, mainly of youngsters and students, lining up to see this controversial artist. A debate was promised on the exhibition by the Ministry of Culture but it was cancelled, and a few days later the whole exhibition was cancelled. This meant that the powers that be, the CPSU, had decided against the exhibition, overruling even the Ministry of Culture.

An artist outside the union can even be accused and sentenced as a "parasite." Take the Joseph Brodsky case. Here, a young poet and translator has actually been sentenced to several years in exile because he tried to exist as a writer outside the writers' union. He earned his living by manual work. When he had saved enough to live on for a while, he would leave his job and get on with his poetry or his translations until he needed more money. Then he would go to work again. But it seems he earned the enmity of certain influential circles in Leningrad, both in the Party and in the Leningrad Union of Writers, in which there was also an element of anti-Semitism. He was arrested, tried, condemned as a "parasite," and exiled to a distant northern province.

In no case of any writer being attacked by the Party has any Soviet writers' union defended its member, not in the days of the Stalin terror nor under Khrushchev. One would have imagined that with the tragedy of so many murdered writers and poets in the Union of Soviet Writers the union would now at least try to protect any writer from injustice. It does not—although all honor must be paid to individual Soviet artists who do. For example, Paustovsky, Shostakovitch, Akhmatova, and others protested over the Brodsky case, and added to this came protests from the European Community of Writers and the International P.E.N. Club. As a result of this pressure, I

xii   *The Poet in Russia*

understand Brodsky has now been released. But the Leningrad Union of Writers joined in attacking him as untalented and consequently not worthy to be a member of the only trade union he is eligible for. In other words, the Party caucus had so decided, and that is the one boss.

Very much in the news of late have been the names Andrei D. Sinyavsky and Yuli M. Daniel, two members of the Union of Soviet Writers who were arrested by the KBG. Sinyavsky is a well-known critic, who wrote the introduction to the latest Russian edition of Pasternak; Daniel is a lesser known writer. Both men were tried and convicted of the charge of smuggling out material severely criticizing Soviet society and publishing it in the West under pseudonyms. (Sinyavsky apparently used the name Abram Tertz and Daniel used Nikolai Arzhak.) Their arrest and trial were highly publicized both in the Soviet Union and abroad. They were convicted of the charges and sentenced to seven years (Sinyavsky) and five years (Daniel) at hard labor. A storm of protest arose from Western writers, publishers, and intellectuals, including Western Communists, and there were indications that individual Soviet citizens expressed strong disapproval of the trial—a protest demonstration was conducted outside the scene of the proceedings. But not one word in defense or support of the two writers has come from the Union of Soviet Writers.

One can think of many other examples. Only three years ago the most popular play in the Soviet Union was *The Island of Aphrodite,* written by a Greek civil-war emigré, Alexis Parnis, who had studied and worked in the Soviet Union. Parnis' play, according to the official charts, was being played in over 250 theatres throughout the length and breadth of the Soviet Union. *Suddenly, one day, that same play disappeared from all those theatres simultaneously!* And Parnis' new play, scheduled for production, was withdrawn. This was at a time when the old producer-actors, Ohklopkov and Cherkassov, were proudly boasting to me that theatres had got back their old autonomy, as in the twenties, and that they could now choose their own repertoire without having to get the approval of the Ministry or the Party. Yet, one command from the Center, and one play disappeared from 250 cities on the theatrical map overnight, and not a word is said—anywhere! The Union of Soviet Writers didn't lift a finger—although individual members expressed their sympathy.

Finally, let me give a personal example of such methods of overriding even the most important organizations by backstage Party control. In 1960 I was invited to be a delegate to the conference on Taras Shevchenko, celebrating his birth, at Kiev. In the course of this conference delegates from various countries pointed out that Shevchenko was practically unknown in the English-speaking world, or indeed outside the Ukraine. I was, accordingly, asked officially by the chairman of the Taras Shevchenko anniversary committee of the Ukraine Academy of Sciences, the famous Ukrainian poet Mikola Bazhan, to take on the task of producing an English translation of selected poems. After many discussions, Mikola Bazhan indicated to me the poems he thought should be translated. As editor, I could use other translations than my own—the basic question was one of quality. Well, it is a very difficult and indeed onerous task to translate from the Ukrainian of Taras Shevchenko. He is not only a great poet, as well as a great artist, but writes in a language that is little known or studied. Therefore, I set about the task even before I received any formal contract. Later I was informed that the contract would be made with me by a Soviet publishing organization then known as the Publishing House in Foreign Languages in Moscow. While waiting to hear from them, I continued my work on the project. Six months passed. Then I had a letter asking if I would please confirm in writing that I was willing to be the translator and editor of the selected works of Taras Shevchenko for the Centenary of 1964. I wrote back and said, yes, of course, this I had agreed to long ago with the Ukraine Academy of Sciences, but would they please make out a formal contract with the usual arrangements, advance, etc.? I heard nothing for another six months. And then came a surprise. A letter from the same organization stated that now, owing to the lapse of time since the original discussions, it would not be possible for me to edit the book abroad. They would have it edited by a Soviet editor in Moscow —but would I be willing, nevertheless, to do my translations? I had already translated so many poems that I had to go through with it. Despite my protests both at the Soviet embassy in London and to the Ukraine Academy of Sciences in Kiev, despite the fact that I had been proposed by the chairman of the Taras Shevchenko committee and approved by the Academy of Sciences, the decision was that this Moscow publishing house would go ahead and put their own editor in charge in Moscow. The result was as I expected: among good translations were included poor translations by Soviet citizens who did not know the English language sufficiently to translate poetry. There were many mistakes and bowdlerizations.[2] However, the position was quite clear that in Moscow, backstage, the Party had decided that they would not let the editorship of this book go out of their control. Overruled were the decisions of experts of the Ukraine Academy of Sciences and of an important Communist statesman and poet like Mikola Bazhan.

In 1962 I was lucky to be in Moscow at the famous One Day of Poetry meeting at the Palace of Sport, which was packed to overflowing with over 14,000 people. I had been invited by the Union of Soviet Writers to read my translations of Russian poets at this great meeting. All the leading poets were billed to appear from all the generations, from Bezymensky to Yevtushenko, Voznesensky, and Akhmadulina. On my way with some of the poets to this meeting, I learned that there was apprehension that the younger poets would not be there. Yevtushenko was still in Cuba and unable to get a plane, and they didn't know where to get hold of Voznesensky. They said these were the poets that would be demanded by the audience. And so it turned out. During the meeting the chairman asked the audience for questions and suggestions to be put in writing and sent up to the desk of the Presidium. Of course, even a small percentage of 14,000 meant hundreds and hundreds of notes! Eventually, practically the whole of the Presidium was engaged in and sorting out these notes, and it was found that the bulk of them were questions about three poets: "Why isn't Voznesensky here?" "Why isn't Yevtushenko here?" and "Why isn't Bulat Okudjava here?" "Who is pre-

---

[2] Later confirmed by the review of this book in the *Times Literary Supplement,* Nov. 6, 1965.

venting them from speaking?" "Who is stopping them from being present?" etc. Then Voznesensky turned up, much to the relief of the Presidium. Akhmadulina was also there, but Yevtushenko of course couldn't get there and there was no news of Bulat Okudjava. However, proceedings went on—my reading of my translations of Mayakovsky was warmly received—but only when the younger poet Voznesensky read his poems did the audience really show excitement. He received an ovation. It was quite clear that up till then the massive audience was not in sympathy with the bulk of the poets performing. This could be told, also, from many other questions that were put in; for example, to the younger poets, someone wrote, "Why are you sitting with those s.o.b. Stalinists? Why aren't you protesting their presence on the platform?" However, it was indicative of the new spirit of freedom and passion that this great stadium was jammed just to hear poets. And so tremendous was the pressure and so electric the atmosphere that I know the Presidium was worried that there might be some overt demonstration. The Presidium's attitude is borne out by the fact that there has been no repetition of such a vast meeting. The next time I was there for this One Day of Poetry, in 1963 and 1964, I found that the meetings had been split up into various clubs in different parts of Moscow, but there was no great central meeting. That speaks for itself of the pressure and the power of poetry in Soviet society.

Some readers may wonder why I go into such detail, or bother to explain what appears to be obvious to everybody. Unfortunately, I find that many people in the West equate their own circumstances with those of their opposite numbers in the Soviet Union. This does not do justice to the facts. And it is against this background that the work of Voznesensky and Yevtushenko and like-minded poets must be understood.

Let me explain a little about that specific background.

Recently I read a poem by an older poet, an important Party member, Yevgeny Dolmatovsky, who has been, so to speak, on the orthodox wing of the writers. Following the Party's admitting to the

Stalinist years of terror, he has been forced to face up to the accusations of the younger generation (his own son, I believe).

Here is a literal translation of his poem:

A DIFFICULT CONVERSATION (1962)[3]

Not having known that sorrow, fortunately,
which from childhood lived in me,
you say:
>*"For how long you lied*
and burned your spirit with baseness,
a good thing it wasn't burnt to ashes.
The burden of Iron Monuments
is overthrown and swept away,
and, so it seems, the time has come
to add to the complex theorem
the final missing link,
and to declare that, now, at last
we shall begin to tell the truth."

.   .   .   .   .

Such tragedies the world has never seen,
and from them one cannot hide in silence.

The one outstanding thing to remember, therefore, is that the majority of the older Soviet artistic intelligentsia, directly or indirectly, knew suffering under Stalinism—in all forms, from the mildest to the most ruthless, from frustration, silence, suppression, ostracism, to false denunciations, frame-ups, imprisonment, concentration camps, hunger, torture, and ignominious deaths.

Now the younger generation, the sons, are divided into two camps, those whose families suffered and those who managed to survive unscathed. On analysis it will be found that many of the present wave of Soviet writers, poets in particular, have felt the effect of the Stalinist period in their own families and directly or indirectly

---

[3] Y. Dolmatovsky, *Poems About Us* (Soviet Writers Publishing House, Moscow), 1964, p. 13.

have felt the suffering. To some it happened when they were very young. For example, Robert Rozhdestvensky, in the latest annual anthology, *One Day of Poetry, 1964*,[4] writes in a poem entitled "Winter '38" how his father comes home from work; the family expects him to react as usual to the evening meal, but instead he smashes his hand on the bedstead and cries:

> *"They are not guilty, not one of them is guilty!"*
> *"What's he talking about, Mother? Father is crying! Why?*
> *He's so strong! He's so big! Who could be bigger than he?"*
> *Mother says*
> *"Quiet"*
>   *and repeats*
>   *"My God, they may hear us!"*
>   *"Who will hear us?"*
> *At that time I was seven years old. I don't remember*
> *any more.*
>   *Tracts of time die out, it was some time before I*
>   *understood my father's cry.*
>   *Only after twenty years.*

Incidentally, this question of fathers and sons had been dealt with in a new film called *The Ilyich Gate*. However, before it could be released, it was banned by Khrushchev and the Party because it was considered an attack on the older generation. Since Khrushchev's retirement it has been released. In one scene, the hero meets the ghost of his father, who had been killed in the last war. He asks his father to give him advice on how to live. The father asks his son how old he is. The son replies, "Twenty-three," and then the father says to him, "Well, I'm only twenty-one myself, how can I advise you?" and disappears.

Take the case of the young poet Vsevelod Bagritsky, son of the famous poet Edward Bagritsky, one of Russia's finest Revolutionary poets. The son was killed at the front in 1942. His book of diaries

---

[4] *One Day of Poetry, 1964* (Soviet Writers Publishing House, Moscow), 1964.

and poems has been published posthumously,[5] with a preface by Michael Svetlov, who says, "The fate of Vsevelod was a hard one. He lost his father when he was twelve years of age. He was fifteen when his mother was unjustly arrested. A year later his beloved brother committed suicide. Vsevelod with bitterness wrote: 'Soon I shall be eighteen years of age, but I've already seen so much sorrow, so much sadness, so much human suffering that sometimes I want to say to people, and indeed to myself: What are we living for, friends? . . .' "

And in his diary, not long before his death as a soldier, the young poet writes, "I don't want very much—just the right to write, think, and speak freely and loudly . . ." and, "I want to defeat the Germans in this war and more so the Committee for Art Affairs, in order that no bureaucrat shall prevent our working." His voice was a harbinger of the generation of Yevtushenko and Voznesensky.

Now let us take Yevtushenko and his wife. His two grand-fathers were both innocent victims of Stalinism—one a veteran revolutionary Red Army commander, the other an author of Soviet textbooks; one was a peasant, the other an intellectual. Both were murdered under Stalin. His wife's grandfather, Shumyatsky, at one time Stalin's head of cinematography, was also eventually arrested and executed, and her father, who worked in radio, was exiled. Her mother was also brought in for cross-examination. This is reflected in his poem "I am older myself . . ."[6]

Apart from that, in his autobiography Yevtushenko mentions many poets he knew who had suffered injustices. This is inevitably the environment of the so-called angry young poet of Russia. Yevtushenko himself dislikes the label "angry young man," because, as he has written, "Russia's poets were always fighters for justice. . . . Her poets helped Russia to think. Her poets helped Russia to struggle against her tyrants." Voznesensky deals directly with this aspect in his poem "The Ballad of the Full-Stop" (p. 5) and, parabolically, in "The Masters" (p. 20).

---

[5] V. Bagritsky, *Diaries, Letters, Poems* (Soviet Writers Publishing House, Moscow), 1964.

[6] *Yevtushenko: Selected Poems*, trans. by Herbert Marshall (Dutton, New York), 1966.

Those who lived under the shadow of the Stalinist period developed a built-in reflex which protected a person from saying or even thinking heretical thoughts, although every now and then the agony of suppressed pain and anger burst through. To this day in my ears rings the cry of agony of that talented Ukrainian poet Andrey Malyshko, a dedicated Party member.

It happened I was in Kiev when his fiftieth birthday was being officially celebrated, and I was invited to attend and read some translations of his poems, which I had already made. It was the usual ceremonious program with the usual official representatives of the State and the Party, during which the poet was presented with the Order of Lenin and congratulations from the Central Committee of the Party and of the Government. The poet responded with thanks and praise for the Party and the Government and what they had done for him. The next evening I attended his own private celebration. The food and drink was, as always, generous and flowing. As the evening went on, more and more of those present were getting tight by continually toasting each other, in the Russian fashion, making short speeches, and then toasting again. Malyshko from time to time replied to the speeches, and then toward the end he suddenly burst out with a cry: *Moyevo mladshevo brata ubila Sovietskaya vlast!* which in translation means, "My youngest brother was killed by Soviet power!" *Nyevinny on byl! Nyevinny!* "He was innocent! Innocent!" At this he broke down and sobbed aloud. There was dead silence in the hall. Soberness suddenly returned at the sound of that poet's cry of agony as he repeated, "My brother was killed by Soviet power." In his poems, as far as I have seen, there isn't one reflection of this personal tragedy. Such is the built-in reflex of the generation of Stalin's day.

The generation born since the war, however, does not have this built-in inhibition.[7] Those of the older generation, though aware that de-Stalinization has taken place, still, every now and again, look over their shoulders, thinking, "But it could come back!" In the younger generation this does not exist, and they speak out quite frankly. The

[7] See the opening lines of Yevtushenko's "Hey Citizens!" in *Yevtushenko: Selected Poems* (Dutton, New York), 1966.

effect on the older generation is very much like that of a Victorian schoolteacher being talked to by a modern beatnik. This new generation wants to try and express itself in every possible way. Yevtushenko said that he chose poetry because "Poetry has mobility. To begin with, a poem is much quicker to write than a novel, and it can be read in public even before it comes out in print. So I chose the public platform as the battlefield from which to defend my views."[8]

Voznesensky already in his first book, *Mosaic,* had written:

> *An artist firstborn—*
> *Is always a tribune.*
> *In him the spirit of overturning,*
> *And rebellion—eternal.* (p. 20)

Nowadays anybody can extemporize a poem on a platform, where it can be taken down on tape recorders and then multiplied by hand. Even though it may not be published at once, or ever, it goes the rounds. That is another reason why the young flock to poetry readings.

Yevtushenko writes about his friend the sculptor Ernst Nyeizvestny: "These artists were older than myself and had fought and been wounded several times at the front. After the war they had refused to become the blind followers of the established academic style and went eagerly in search of new art forms. They thought, with some justification, that they had shed their blood for the right to paint and sculpt as they liked, but not everyone saw their point of view and my friends were having a hard time . . ."

It is reported that at the meeting of the Ideological Commission of the Central Committee, when Nyeizvestny was attacked for unpatriotic "Formalist" art, Yevtushenko defended him, saying, "Nyeizvestny came back from the war, his body criss-crossed with wounds; I hope he will live many more years and produce many more fine works of art."

"As people say," Khrushchev retorted, "only the grave corrects a hunchback." Yevtushenko answered: "I hope we have outlived the

---

[8] Y. Yevtushenko, *A Precocious Autobiography* (Dutton, New York, and Collins, London), 1963, p. 96.

time when the grave was used as a means of correction." Such an answer would have been utterly impossible in the days gone by. The irony of this is underlined by Voznesensky's poem on Nyeizvestny (p. 120), written after Khrushchev's downfall.

Yet the battle against the conservative, pro-Stalinist element still goes on. As I write I hear that Yevtushenko recited a poem at the Moscow celebration of Yesenin's seventieth birthday (if he had lived!) that attacked the Komsomol (Young Communist League) for trying "to knead poets like wax." The General Secretary, who was present, stormed out protesting—but no official action was taken.[9] It is important to realize that the Party was angered at Yevtushenko for publishing his autobiography abroad not primarily because of its contents but because it was published without Party approval. It can be a crime against the State to do so. That was the charge made against the recently arrested and convicted Sinyavsky and Daniel.

Linked up with this is also the very human element of professional jealousy. Many of the older writers are bitterly envious of Yevtushenko's and Voznesensky's personal success abroad. For the young writers who visit the West today make a sharp contrast with members of past Soviet cultural delegations, always with a political Commissar somewhere around, checking everything they said, everywhere they went, and everyone they met. Soviet writers used to meet only with Communist Party organizations, or fellow-travellers, or Government officials and held meetings where only stereotyped answers were given and no direct questions were allowed from the floor. All questions had to be written down and censored by the chairman. The Soviet writers were usually not allowed to visit private homes, and they could never admit truths about their own regime, whatever their personal feelings. But when Yevtushenko and Voznesensky visited the West, they went about on their own, visited any place they wanted to, answered questions without hindrance, and ad-

---

[9] Since writing I read that Yevtushenko had been drafted into the Army, though he is thirty-two. It transpired he had never served his obligatory National Service. But, on the other hand, both he and Voznesensky have been made candidates for the Lenin Prize!

mitted two sides to a question. On top of that, they passionately and brilliantly recited poetry that had something fresh and honest to say. It was no longer mere propaganda, but genuine poetry, and it was addressed to humanity, not just to a limited class or party.

Finally, there are simply the vested interests. It is now admitted that huge quantities of books of poetry lie unsold in Soviet warehouses,[10] whereas Yevtushenko and Voznesensky are not only sold in editions of 50,000 and 100,000 but are resold secondhand at higher prices! All this, as well as their poetic attacks on Stalin's heirs, creates a lot of powerful enemies.

They have also been attacked in poetry by the older generation. For example, Sergei Vasiliev wrote an epigram called "Different Wants of Yevgeny Yevtushenko" in the anthology *One Day of Poetry, 1963,* which I roughly translate as follows:

I want—under the guise of struggling with the cult of personality,
my own personality, with special urgency
to garland with paper roses.
I want self-advertisement, poster-placard size,
oh la la
     and with all this hubbub even my very own mother
I want to poison.

Another poet, this time a contemporary, Vladimir Firsov (who, I am told, is simply jealous of Yevtushenko and Voznesensky because of the attention they get), wrote a poem to his Aunt Polya in *One Day of Poetry, 1963,* in which he sentimentalizes her hard life as a mother feeding her children, who are now building great Soviet constructions everywhere, and he ends up with these lines:

> *Aunty Polya, my dear one,*
> *your good tender hands have fed everyone,*
> *those in the pits, those in the textile factories,*

---

[10] N. Koryavin, "Why Do People Write Poetry," *Yunost* ("Youth"), No. 5, 1962, p. 72.

those on construction in Siberia.
Have fed even poets,
who are indifferent to your hands.
Those poets who write verses
about boulevard guitars
and about the last trolley bus,
who take in boys from the deserted streets.
Aunt Polya, my dear one,
forgive them!

Now, of course, anybody who knows Soviet poetry, will recognize that this is an attack, particularly on Yevtushenko, Voznesensky,[11] and Bulat Okudjava, who accompanies his poetry with a guitar. During a meeting of the Union of Soviet Writers, Firsov actually demanded that Yevtushenko not only be censured for publishing his autobiography abroad, but be tried for treason and sentenced to the highest penalty, death! Firsov's demand was indignantly rejected, however, by the majority.

But since Khrushchev's retirement, the barometer does seem to be setting toward fair. At the recent election of a new executive for the Moscow section, the writers' union threw out most of the old guard members and chose many prominent younger writers and liberals, including Yevgeny Yevtushenko. Writers who for some reason or another had been considered the heirs of Stalin were taken off the ballot list during the preliminary discussion. Following Khrushchev's enforced retirement, Ilyitchov, the main enemy of the young poets in the Central Committee of the Party, in charge of its Ideological Commission, was removed. In his place the new man, Demichev, indicated that things would be better than under Mr. Khrushchev. This was, however, followed by attacks from the old guard on the two "liberal" magazines, *Yunost* and *Novy Mir,* and in particular against Yevtushenko and Voznesensky, as well as Solzhenitsyn, Aksyonov (whose father was executed under Stalin), and Arbuzov.

---

11 See his poems, "The Last Trolley Bus" (p. 18) and "The Guitar" (p. 51).

Since then, we have read the State newspaper *Izvestia* defending the old guard criticisms and the Party newspaper *Pravda* coming out and attacking its sister paper with a 5,000-word essay by its editor, saying, "The Party's wish is to defend the artist's freedom to choose theme and subject, style and manner of execution." So it looks as if at long last the Party is being forced to return to its pre-Stalin artistic freedom at least.

In addition to the foregoing problems facing original and honest poets in the Soviet Union, it seems that Russian poets have in them, in the very nature of their being and their environment, a tragic inevitability, a fate which seems to dog them, irrespective of the regime they live under, whether they fight for it or against it. One has only to consider the number of poets in Russia who were killed at an early age, either by their own hand, or by sickness and privation, or by a stupid accident, or by their own government.[12] In Tsarist Russia Ryleyev was executed at thirty-one. Batushrov went mad at thirty-six. Venevitinov died at twenty-two, Delvig at thirty-two. Griboyedov was killed at thirty-four. Chaadayev, though sane, was incarcerated in a lunatic asylum by the Tsar. Pushkin was shot in a duel at thirty-seven, Lermontov in a duel at twenty-six. In Soviet Russia, Yesenin (twenty-nine), Mayakovsky (thirty-seven), Tsvetayeva, Yashvili, Dementiev, Egishe Charentse, Fadeyev, and others committed suicide. Gumilyov was shot for opposing the regime. Khlebnikov starved to death.[13] Alex Blok died in spiritual and physical agony. Mandleshtam, Perets Markish, Itzik Pfeffer, Titian Tabidze, Sergei Tretyakov, B. Kornilov (the husband of the Leningrad poetess Olga Bergholtz), V. Narbut, Chernyavsky, Filiansky, T. Gamzai,

---

[12] It is indicative that Chekhov's tragic "comedy" *The Seagull* ends with the act of a poet who shoots himself. "Those whom the gods love die young"—particularly in Russia.

[13] Victor Shklovsky writing on the tragic death of Khlebnikov said: "Forgive us for yourself and for others that we murder . . ."

Mayakovsky cried: "After the death of Khlebnikov various newspapers and journals printed articles about Khlebnikov, filled with sympathy. I read them with revulsion. When, finally, will these comedies of posthumous cures end?! Where were these writers, when the living Khlebnikov, spat upon by critics, passed through Russia alive? I know others still living, maybe not the equals of Khlebnikov, but who await the same end." See my *Mayakovsky* (Hill and Wang, New York, and Dobson, London), 1965, p. 33.

Ch. Begizove, Vorony father and son, Yusuf, Erlich Wolfe, and so many others, were all executed by the regime, which they had fought for and were part of. Olga Bergholtz, Leonid Martynov, Halkin, N. Zabolotsky, B. Ruchyov, Smelyakov, Victor Bokov, Elena Vladimirova, Aldan-Semyonov, Joseph Brodsky, and scores of others were imprisoned or exiled. The poet-philosopher A. Yesenin-Volpin (a natural son of the famous poet) was put into a lunatic asylum by both the Stalin and Khrushchev regimes. And there are those who were just persecuted by having their works suppressed: Pasternak, Akhmatova, and many others. So this peculiar tragic fate is something that must be pondered and taken into account when reading Russian poetry.

Today's poets are very much aware of the fate that has dogged their predecessors. "The fate of almost every Russian poet has been tragic," writes Yevtushenko. Yevtushenko indeed ends his great poem "Bratsky GES" with a particular chapter on Mayakovsky and his fate; Voznesensky writes passionately about it in "Mayakovsky in Paris" (p. 97) and in his notes to *The Triangular Pear* quotes Marx, "Poets are in need of great endearment" (which, incidentally, Anatole Lunacharsky also quoted on the suicide of Mayakovsky— but to no avail).

Two passionate poems have been dedicated to Titian Tabidze, the Georgian Mayakovsky, a Communist, a fine poet, a sincere Soviet patriot who was beloved of so many other poets and writers who knew him. One is by Bulat Okudjava, like Yevtushenko and Voznesensky a poet beloved by Soviet youth, and the other by a young, almost unknown woman poet, Yunna Morits. I was present when Bulat Okudjava gave an evening recital to the members of a Soviet economics institute. He prefaced his reading of this poem by saying, "This poem is dedicated to Titian Tabidze, unjustly executed in 1938. The names of his executioners have not yet been established." And then he read "Guard and Protect Us Poets":

Guard and protect us poets, guard and protect us, we cry.
A century's left, a half, a year, now a week, an hour goes by,

three minutes, two, the seconds tick, four, three, two, one, zero falls.
Guard and protect us poets—so that one should be for all.

Guard and protect us, with our sins, our joys, without, early, late,
for our Dantes,[14] young and handsome, always lies in wait.
Curses he's not forgotten for the deed he long has done,
but alas his destined calling demands he load his gun.

For our Martynov's[15] crying, remembering blood he shed before.
Once already he has killed—nor wants to kill once more.
But his destiny is such, the bullet's die is cast,
thus the twentieth century will summon him at last.

Guard and protect us poets from the hands of fools and knaves,
from far too hasty judgments, from friends so blind, oh, save.
Guard and protect us poets, while to preserve there's time.
Only do not preserve us, so we lay our bones in lime.

Only do not protect us, as wolfhounds hunters guard.
Only do not protect us, as hunters guard the Tsar.
Then for you poems will be written, songs sung unendingly.
Only protect and guard us poets—let us protected be.

Once all this has been said, however, it must be clearly understood that subject to the stern conditions I have outlined, the lot of the artist in the Soviet Union has many features to be envied and emulated. His status in society is of the highest, he is well paid, he is not a Bohemian odd man out, he is an honored and respected member of society, whose work and experience is highly valued. Colossal sums are spent by the State and its subsidiary organizations on subsidizing art, in all its forms. Sums that make state support and patronage in Great Britain and the United States look very small indeed. On the artist that conforms, honors of every kind are conferred—and that is true of any society—except in the Soviet Union it is on a grand scale. The Lenin Prize means not only about $16,000 cash, but priority to

---

[14] Dantes was the provocateur who shot the poet Pushkin in a duel.
[15] Martynov shot the poet Lermontov, also in a duel.

acquire scarce goods like a car, an apartment, space at holiday resorts, etc.

In the field of literature, writing and translating poetry are professions. Soviet organizations pay me the highest rates for my translations of Russian poetry into English, far more than any other country in the world. In no other country in the world can a man earn a living just as a poet or a translator of poetry. In our world he has always to do it on the side. In no other country are there such large printings of books of poetry, Yevtushenko: 100,000; Voznesensky: 60,000; Mayakovsky is published in millions. Poetry appears in practically every journal and newspaper, including the Party organ *Pravda* and the State organ *Izvestia.* The popular youth magazine *Yunost,* of which Yevtushenko is on the editorial board, issues 1,600,000 copies a month, with ten to twelve pages of poetry in each issue. Halls are packed at poetry readings, from 500 to 1,000 in the small clubs up to the 14,000 who came to the Palace of Sport in 1962.

Two years ago a Theatre of Reciters and Poets was founded, under the auspices of the Art Workers Club, in Moscow. Every week special concerts devoted to poetry are given, with both reciters and poets participating. The Chief Director of the Theatre, George Sorokin, is himself a talented professional reciter, another profession practically unknown in our society. A few months ago at the Moscow Theatre of Reciters and Poets, leading Soviet poets of all generations read one of their poems in the original, and in turn I read my translations, from Gorky to Yevtushenko and Voznesensky. The theatre was filled, although it was hot that evening and half the program was in English. This Theatre of Poets also appears regularly on television. Invited to read some of my translations of Mayakovsky, I was told afterward that in this program I had had an audience of 40,000,000 in an all-union tie-up, from Tallin to Vladivostok.

Thus, the breaking of the iron burden of Stalinism, however incomplete, has allowed a growth of poetry that is unique. Today interesting poets are writing in every language of the Soviet Union, though we know so little as yet of what is being written in those many languages. (I, alas, can only cope with the Russian and the Ukrainian, but I hope that some others will take up the translation of poets from the many other national languages.)

And another extraordinary phenomenon is the presence of so many first-class women poets. This is something quite unparalleled, and yet not always realized by the powers that be in the Soviet Union. Indeed, I once had a discussion with the now Prime Minister, Mr. Kosygin, in which I mentioned the large number of women poets, and he did not seem to think it significant. I had to point out that in the history of literature the number of women poets was very small: Sappho, Elizabeth Barrett Browning, Emily Dickinson, Edna St. Vincent Millay, etc. Now, of course, there are more women poets in the modern world, but nowhere are there so many superb women poets as now writing in the Soviet Union.

Finally, let me make it quite clear that any conclusions or theories I have outlined here or in my notes are entirely my own and not the poets'.

Let there be no mistake about it—Andrey Voznesensky and Yevgeny Yevtushenko are passionate patriots of their people and their country. Despite the crimes and blunders committed by the Party and its bureaucratic State apparatus, despite the tragedy of Stalinism, and despite the Philistine hangover that still has to be fought, the post-Stalin generation realizes that its people created a new society in the Soviet Union. The Soviet people suffered both in peace and war, from their own Stalin and from Hitler, but they conquered and survived both. Deep are the wounds that were inflicted, colossal were the tragic losses, in people, goods, wealth, happiness, and ideals. Out of this holocaust arise artists like Yevtushenko and Voznesensky, fighting "for fathers' truths against fathers' lies," fighting against "barbarians of all times," fighting against the dogmatists, the heirs of Stalin, the *apparatchiki* ("Party hacks"), the outdated slogans, and shallow black-and-white "socialist-realism." They are proud of what their people have done, despite all this.

Despite all this, they realize that the only possible future for their own people and the rest of the world is in peaceful coexistence.

Yevtushenko writes: "In the final analysis, humanity has only two ways out—either universal destruction or universal brotherhood." And the key to this lies above all, he says, in the relationship between the Russian and American peoples.

I couple the names of Yevtushenko and Voznesensky for a special reason—together they sum up the outlook and contradictions of the post-Stalinist period and at the same time reflect two complementary trends in Russian poetry. Yevtushenko still remembers the shock and trauma of de-Stalinization and its effect on Soviet youth; the whole history of his family and that of his wife's is typical. He started writing poetry for a newspaper in his teens,[16] whereas Voznesensky didn't come into print until he was thirty. And it seems Voznesensky has not had such intimate contact with the victims of the Stalin period. This is what perhaps partly causes the difference in the style of the two poets: Yevtushenko stems from Nekrassov and Mayakovsky; Voznesensky from Blok and Pasternak.

Yevtushenko's poems narrate, follow through a subject in a traditional way, attacking his object of criticism head on, using simple images. Voznesensky projects a montage of conflicting images and metaphors and allusions, without a narrative line or an overt connection; in other words, he is more subjective, his style closer to the modern Western generation. Nevertheless, it would be a distortion to translate him in "hip" style completely, using the sexual license now permitted in the West, or to equate him with the beatnik school of poetry in America. One translator has tried to do that, but it gives a false impression of the original. Soviet poetry may come to that style eventually, but the Party's puritan tradition is still strong, however hypocritical it may be. Party critics are still attacking Voznesensky for his "obscurity" and "murkiness" and "subjectivity." And indeed he compares himself to Joan Miró and his "hypnotic paintings" and "disquieting fantasy"[17] and to Goya, of the "Disasters of War" etchings. Yevtushenko's conception of the poet is as a soldier,

---

[16] His first book of poems, *Prospectors of the Future,* was published in 1952.
[17] His newest book is called *Anti-Worlds* and the poem with this title is a fantasy worthy of Miró.

much like Mayakovsky's; but Voznesensky's poet is an "accoucheur of the new" and is as "unexpected as poker-chips fall."

The impact of modern science on the younger generation of today is clearly seen in Voznesensky's work. He himself is the son of a scientist, brought up in a highly cultured and sophisticated environment. The world of atomic science, computers, space rockets, the atomic and hydrogen bombs, and cosmonauts is clearly reflected in his work. Voznesensky's poetry not only brings in scientific allusions but actual mathematical formulae. He finds his self-portrait in a New York airport, as Mayakovsky found his in Brooklyn Bridge.[18]

Voznesensky faces up to the great conflicts of his times and cries out:

> *The times spat at me.*
> *I spit back at the times again.*

He finds a parallel between Negroes in the States and poets in the USSR:

> *We are Negroes, we are poets,*
> > *within us spin the planets.*
> *Thus we lie, like sacks, with stars and legends stacked. . . .*
>
> *When we are kicked about,*
> *The firmament rebels.*
> *Under your jackboots*
> *The Universe yells!* (page 45)

and on seeing the Guggenheim Museum, "the swan song of Frank Lloyd Wright's genius," Voznesensky recognizes a design he had worked on as an architectural student and says, "I ponder with joy on the unity of human fantasy."

HERBERT MARSHALL

Southern Illinois University
Carbondale, Illinois
December, 1965

---

[18] H. Marshall, *Mayakovsky* (Hill and Wang, New York, and Dobson, London), 1965, p. 336.

Mosaic

A PARABOLIC BALLAD

Fate, like a rocket, flies in a parabola
Usually in gloom—more rarely along a rainbow.

Once there lived a fiery-ginger artist Gauguin,
A bohemian, but in time past a stock-broker.
To get into the royal Louvre
                    from Montmartre,

He made
          a detour through Java and Sumatra!
Upwards he soared, forgetting the madness of money,
The cackle of wives, academies stuffy,
earth's gravitational pull
                    overcoming.

Over beer mugs high-priests wag laughing:
"A straight line's shorter, steeper the parabola's ascent,
Wouldn't it be better to copy the heavenly tent?"

But he speeded on, a rocket transporting
Through the winds, ripping coat-tails and ears.
And entered the Louvre not through the main portal—
By an angry
          parabola
                    through the ceiling he pierced!

The brave to their truths by different ways go travelling,
A maggot—through a hole, a man—through a parabola.

Once upon a time a girl lived next door to me.
Together we studied, together exams we passed.

How far **I** went!

What the hell transported **me**
Between massive ambiguous Tbilisi stars!

Forgive me for that parabola perverse.
In dark hallways embrace shoulders shivering. . . .
Oh, how you rang in the murk of the universe
A taut and straight antenna rod quivering!
But I still fly on,

then land by its aid—
Earthy and frozen, by your call-sign made.
How hard to achieve is that parabola! . . .

Wiping away canons, prognoses, paragraphs,
Surges on art

love

and history—
Along a parabolic trajectory!

He sets off for Siberia this very night[1]

   .   .   .   .   .

And, maybe, after all, the shortest's—a straight line?

---

[1] The printed version reads: "Galoshes drown in the Siberian spring . . ." but
the poet altered the line in his reading.

THE BALLAD OF THE FULL-STOP[1]

"A ballad? About a full-stop?! About a deadly pillule?!"
Blockhead!
You've forgotten about Pushkin's bullet![2]

That the winds whistled, as through the stops of clarionets,
Through the bullet-ridden heads of our finest poets.

With a shot piercing petty tyranny and pomposity
The trajectory of their whistle flew to posterity!
And there was no full-stop. But there was—a start.

As through station doors, into earth we depart.

And black as a muzzle is the full-stop of the tunnel . . .
Leading to immortality?
Or to oblivion's funnel? . . .

There's no death. No full-stop. There's the bullet's trajectory—
The same straight line's secondary projection.

There's no full-stop in the estimate of nature.
We'll be immortal.
                    And that's for sure!

---

[1] This is an echo from an early poem of Mayakovsky's that foreshadowed his suicide; in 1915, in his poem "The Backbone Flute," he wrote:

> More and more I'm thinking—
> wouldn't it be best to place
> the full-stop of a bullet at my ending.

See my *Mayakovsky* (Hill and Wang, New York, and Dobson, London), 1965, p. 28.

[2] The poet Pushkin was shot in a duel. Lermontov similarly was shot in a duel and Mayakovsky shot himself.

RECITAL ON A BUILDING SITE[1]

They intimidate me with formalism.

How far you are from reality,
High-priests, by stinking formalin
And incense impregnated!

In you, maybe, virgin soil is seen
But from you sprouts no magic seed.

Art is deathly without a spark,
Not so much divine as human,—
So that—an impassable jungle dark—
Listen bulldozer crewmen.

They've had it tough and salty,
But to stand as now, themselves,
They—unshaven as the sun and scaly
As pine trees—came out of their shells.

So that a Chuvash maiden chubby—[2]
Brushing away tears of blue,
Brushing away—from a face pure but grubby,
Brushing a tear—as if a dragonfly flew—
From her palms sent hand-claps pealing . . .

Because of this to bear I'm able
Even the most abusive boar-spearing
And the most libellous labels.

---

[1] At the same time as Voznesensky was being called a Formalist he was giving recitals of his poems to workers on the job with great success, in this case to workers on a building site.

[2] *Chuvash:* a people living in the middle reaches of the Volga, in the Chuvash Autonomous Republic.

WHO ARE YOU?

FROM A POEM

Who are we—poker chips or giants?
Genius in the bloodstream of the planets.
No "physicists," no "lyricists" exist—
Just pygmies or poets!

Independent of our works the epoch
Vaccinated us like smallpox.
The flabbergastingly: "Who are you?"
Skids us like a racetrack.

Who are you? Who are you? Then suddenly—no? . . .
On Venus an overcoat's irritating!
Starlings strive their best to crow.
Architects to be poet-creators!

And thawing their palms,
Poetesses run to be pedlars! [1]

But what about you? . . .
How many months is it—
Aiming at the stars, you trudged the puddles.
School finished with, pigtails cut,
Became a salesgirl—then chucked that.

But, between Stoleshnikov[2] kiosks
As if again playing "It,"

---

[1] This is an allusion to Bella Akhmadulina, the poetess.
[2] A Moscow street.

Panting and puffing you stand
A teen-age doll,
        a doe,
                a lovable bitch!

Who are you? Who?!—You look with longing
Into books, windows—but where are you meanwhile?—
You recline, as to a telescope,
To masculine eyes watching immobile. . . .

I wander with you, Vera, Vega! . . .
For, 'midst an avalanche let loose,
I too am an abominable snowman
Absolutely elusive.

THE ARTIST[1]

Letter to K. L. Zelinsky[2]

In this age of barbarism and atoms
We're the accoucheurs of the new.
To us this share of Hades
By morals and custom is due.

Yes—we are the midwives.
But the age roars to the brutal,
Like a cross-breed between a baboon
And an avio-motor.

When such-like are being born
Try if you can to withstand
Being burnt on electrodes,
And holding radium in your hand.

When on to the skeleton excrescent
Grows the spirit-anemone.
Oh, the radio-active basis
Of professional mastery!

    .   .   .   .   .

And in his studio the artist,
Happy with this his lot,
Stands
      immortally
            sick
With the sickness of radial light!

---

[1] This is the shortened version.

[2] A contemporary Soviet literary critic who has written seriously and sympathetically about modern Soviet poetry.

TO VICTOR BOKOV[1]

A poet has no patronym.
Art is adolescence's synonym.

Blue-eyed he passes by,
A balalaika-bard on the wing,
His eyes—like a bass's eyes,
Or a window wide into Spring.

He's as unexpected as poker-chips fall.
As gusty-lusty as March. . . .
A poet has no end at all.
Art—is but the start.

I—AM GOYA!

I—am Goya!
The foe gouged my eyes' craters
                        flying over the naked field.

I—am grief.

I—am the grim voice
Of war, the cinders of cities
                        on the snow fields of '41.

I—am hunger.

I—am the gullet
Of the girl garrotted, whose body tolled like a bell,
                                over the naked square . . .

I—am Goya!

O grapes
Of wrath! In salvoes I soared to the West—
                        I am the ashes of the uninvited guest!
And with strong stars the memorial skies I impaled—
Like nails.

I—am Goya.

THE FOGGY STREET

The suburb is foggy, like a tumbler pigeon.

                              Militiamen like anchor-buoys rock.

The fog is surging.

What century? What epoch?[1]

Everything's in bits, like in a fit of delirium.

                              People as if dismantled. . . .

I wander, querying.

More precisely—I flounder, in cotton-wool mantled.

Parking lights. Noses. Cap-bands posh.

                           As if in a focussing glass double-imaged.

Galoshes?

Mustn't swap noddles in the scrimmage!

So a woman—lips hardly having left

                         is doubled and something resurrecting

No longer a beloved—a widow bereft,

                      still yours—yet a stranger already. . . .

With curbstones and passers-by I contend . . .

                      Venus? An ice-cream vendor goes! . . .

Friends?

Oh, those home-bred Iagos!

             .   .   .   .   .[2]

I survive, stumble, knock,

                         fog, fog—you can't tell,

---

[1] An echo of Pasternak—who asked in one of his poems, "What epoch is it in the courtyard?" He was severely castigated by the Party critics for having dared raise such a question in "the epoch of Communism."

[2] Lines cut in later version.

Whose cheek d'you brush in the fog? . . .
Oh, Hell!
Fog, fog—no one hears. . . .

How wonderful when the fog disappears!

AUTUMN

To S. Schipachov[1]

Ducks' wings flapping and flopping.
And on the paths of the forest darkening
The last brief shimmer of cobwebs,
The last spokes of a bicycle sparkling.

And following the example they give,
At the last house you'll knock for leave-taking.
In that house a woman lives
But for supper no husband's awaited.

She'll fling back the latch for me,
Against my jacket rubbing her cheek,
She'll hold out her mouth laughingly.
And suddenly limp, will understand everything—
Understand the autumnal summons of the fields,
The break-up of families, seed-flight and yield. . . .

Quivering and young
She will think about how
Even the apple tree bears fruit,
A calf is born to the old brown cow.

And that life ferments in the hollow of oaks,
In meadows, in houses, in windswept woods.
For them—to shoot into ears, to bell and troat.
For her—to lament and grieve and brood.

---

[1] Stepan Petrovitch Schipachov (b. 1899), Soviet poet.

How those lips whisper burningly:
"What are my hands, my breasts, my shoulders for?
What do I live for and stoke the stove
And go to my daily chores?"

I take her by the shoulders tight—
I don't know myself what it means at all. . . .

Through the glass the first frost falls
And the fields like aluminum lie.
Across them black—across them grey,
Right up to the railway line
Stretch out tracks of footprints—mine.

THE NEW YEAR TREE[1]

Beyond the windows caryatids,
But in apartments—stiletto heels swing . . .
The New Year trees
                        with wings
                                    reactive
Come seething through the ceiling.

What kind of miracles are prophesied to us?
What kind of charades are here
In this chastity coniferous,
In these fiery spheres?!

O girlie with the mandolin!
Stupefying, rebuking, revealing,
Blazing like a mandarin
Ginger locks unpeeling.

Playing pranks, like a school-kid merry,
Nibbling pine needles green . . .
What will she cherish,
                        what will perish
Of her year to be?

She plays the fool, is filled with fright . . .
Snow thaws outside the room,
And the sweeper there in white
Is like the man on the moon.

---

[1] In Soviet Russia Christmas is not officially celebrated, but New Year's Eve is.
The Russian Orthodox Church's Christmas falls on January 7. The New Year
tree, however, still has its Christmas overtones in Soviet society.

Epochs, goblets, moons weave . . .
"Blow out the candles, blow!"
Love is always—
                    New Year's Eve.

A New Year
            of the soul.

But the rising ferment of fir trees
Like a woman in darkness flits—
All's in the future,
                    as in beads,
And the pine needles on her lips!

THE LAST SUBURBAN TRAIN

Girls with gold fillings, lads with flick knives. . . .
Two conductors like somnolent sphinxes. . . .

Workers sleep inside the car,
The car's in the power of sleep,
But the platform mumbles and jars,
The trolley-arm tipsily sweeps. . . .

I'm travelling on that platform,
Escaping from the heat.
The air drones like a gypsy camp
When guitars and pickpockets meet.

And then it happened somehow,
My poems I started reading
Between broad-shouldered shadows,
Fag-ends, and orange peelings.

They have their own craft and code.
Still I read to them aloud
How a young girl froze
To an icy window snowbound.

A hundred times they've been jailed,
Spat at the highest penalty.[1]
From even the dirtiest deal
They always emerged scot-free.

---

[1] Execution by shooting.

For that girl they don't give a hang?
At my rhymes they simply howl?
They dig this bird with a bang
And powder laid on with a trowel?!

You stand—the devils sleep.
Your blouse reveals at a glance
The whole dactyloscopy
Of lads from a Malakhov[2] band.

Why do you cry so intensely?
And, all lit up with tears,
You whisper to me uncensored—
The purest of words I hear? . . .

Then suddenly the whole car's stunned,
For out of the train appearing,
Along the platform you run
Purer

        than Dante's

                Beatrice.

---

[2] A suburb of Moscow, notorious for its hooligan bands.

THE MASTERS   *A Poem of Seven Headings,*
with a Requiem and Dedications.[1]

FIRST DEDICATION

Belfries of bells, ringers of bells . . .
Peals. Chimes . . .

To you,
Artists
Of all times!

To you,
Michelangelo,
Barma,[2] Dante!
Burned alive to ashes glow
By lightning-flashes of talent.

Your hammers did not hew out
Statues and columns of stone—
They knocked crowns off brows
And shook down thrones.

An artist firstborn—
Is always a tribune.
In him the spirit of overturning,
And rebellion—eternal.

---

[1] This poem concerns the designing and building of St. Basil's Cathedral in Red Square, which in its day was attacked by the Philistines. Legend has it that the Tsar asked the architect if he could build another to equal it and when the architect replied that he could, the Tsar ordered him to be blinded so that no rival could hire him.

[2] Barma (along with Postnik) was the architect of St. Basil's.

Within walls were you immured.
On pyres you were burned.
Monks like brown ants
On your very bones danced.

Art rose in resurrection
From torture and execution
And, flint-like, how it beat
On the stones of Moabit.[3]

Bloody callouses cloyed.
Ashes and sweat.
And the Muse, like Zoya,[4]
To the scaffold they led.

But there are no serums
Against her sacred truth—
Sculptors,
            warriors,
Glory to you!

SECOND DEDICATION

Brothlike Moscow bubbles,
under pealing chimes . . .

To you,
Barbarians
Of all times!

---

[3] Nazi prison in Berlin.
[4] Zoya Kosmodemenskaya, a Soviet heroine of the Second World War who defied her captors till she was hanged.

The tyrants, the Tsars,
In ovoidal tiaras,
In cassocks of auto-da-fé
And gun-muzzle top hats arrayed!

Insuring against fires,
Cash-boxes and empires.
You saw in Pegasus
But a Trojan horse.

The chisel and trowel—your foe.
And burnt-out eyes,
Like firebrands,
Glow
And burn in the nights.

Your condemnation is in my words.
Let there be—shame,
Let there be heard
Curses on your name!

I

Once there lived a Tsar.
And a courtyard had that Tsar.
In that courtyard was a stake.
They plaited not bast on that stake—
They basted men at that stake!

The Tsar was sick, the Tsar was lame,
And rebels and thieves to his palace came.
With a purse unfilled—

Hands are stronger still!
To the village he brings unrest.

To the Tsarina he whistles his behest.

And rapping his scepter,
                the Tsar gave command,
That on Red Square should stand
Out of colored terracotta
A seven-headed cathedral—
A seven-headed dragon.

The Tsar to fortify.
The folk to terrify.

    II

There were seven brave ones,
There were seven strong ones,
From over the seas of aquamarine,
From the far-off northern scene,

Where the lake Ladoga lies,
Where the curving rainbow flies.

A stone foundation firm they laid
Along white curving shores,
So that, like a rainbow made,
Seven cities should soar.

Like a ship's long pennant,
Like the songs of a pedlar.

One—towerlike, purple blent,
Brigandlike, turbulent.
Another like virginity,
Tall and white-breasted.
The third like a sapling tree,
A garden city, green-crested!

Ornament-embellished, brick-wrought,
Shine on the hills . . .
By the bodyguard were they brought,
A new cathedral to build.

III

Curly locks—wood-shavings manes,
Strong hands—on the jack-planes.
Fierce Russian lads,
In red blouses clad.

Eyes—with recklessness filled.
With such strength and will
Watch out or accidental-like
The kingdom may be set alight!

Chuck out, children of hell,
Your trowels and chisels,
Don't cast pearls
Before Dutch tiles. . . .

IV

Not as a mad memorial
Was your cathedral raised,

But as an earthly tribute
In the god of fertility's praise.

Cupolas curved as coconuts,
And pumpkin cupolas are found.
Headdresses of turquoise and rust
Embroider the windows round.

Through the tinsel rind
Scrolls peep out and wind,
Thus in the sixteenth century
Imagined its Michurin.[6]

Savage cabbage heads,
Violent leaves ashiver,
Cockerel feathers red
In nomadic quivers.

And turrets, cork-screw-like
On every side uprise,
And cupolas sprouting spikes
Threaten the very skies!

And Muscovites gave prayers
To such daring work and ardor.
To such melons and maize
In a monstrous garden.

v

Glancing at domes like head-gear
Thus spake the Boyars' will:

---

[6] Famous Russian horticulturist (like Luther Burbank), who bred new strains
of fruit in giant sizes.

"They're the lowest scum here,
They'll be lower still!
Such mother-of-pearl facing—
One could really go crazy.
So sorely agitating
Their red lead and antimony-plating."

The gallant merchant,
Dutch carpetbagger,
Spluttered: "Hey, outrageous,
Blasphemous decorations!

Some craftsmen the Tsar has discovered—
Troublemakers and brigands!
Using not brushes,
But bludgeons!
Seven cities these Antichrists
Have conjured up together.
To them our life's disfranchised,
To them our Russia's no mother!

   . . . And the youngest at that inn,
   A filcher, boasted and bragged,
   That in the night before matins
   This most insolent braggart
   Had kissed the white breasts
   Of the chaste princess. . . ."

And the scribe and his cronies,
Like rats in their corners,
Furtively sniggered and smirked:
"Not a church but a smirch! . . ."

   . . . But the church blazed the horizon
   Like a slogan to insurrection,

Like a flame of anger rising—
A cathedral of sedition!

The deacon jerked back in a funk,
The merchant hid in a trunk.
And the German hopped like a goat,
Hitching up his long black coat.
Of evil you are and vice,
Cathedral of Antichrist! . . .

But watching and whistling the peasant stands.
Stands whistling, stands watching.
Slowly stroking
               his axe with his hand.

VI

Hoarfrost, laughter, horse hoofs beating and the ringing
                                 bark of dogs.
Like devils we worked, but today—let's drink, be gay!
Let's play!
Up with the skirts of the girls—and away!

Hey, on blue, on glazed, yes, on fiery blazing
                             sleds . . .
The cupolas flame like fresh fried eggs, on the wide-open
                               snow-clad steppes.
Yes!—
Only lips on lips!

Past bazaars, past Easter eggs, past jars, and golden carps
                               we're rushing—
Through all the sabled, stabled, tattered, scattered Russias.

Hey!
Hurry! Make your getaway!

Dawns another working day in a thousand different ways.
Hey, carpenters, saw boards to build new cities, whet your blades.

N-e-w cit-ies to be raised?
Maybe better—for coffins to be made? . . .

VII

The dawn is dumb
On prison walls.
But where's the poem?
There's no poem at all.

It had seven headings—
A cathedral seven-domes enskied.
But now its voice is deadened—
Like a face without eyes.

It stands in the night.
A poem at the block.

.   .   .   .

The executioners wipe
Their hands on their smocks.

REQUIEM

No beams you'll be beating, no strolling through meadows
There won't be, there won't be, there won't be any cities!

No patterned towers will float in the mist.
No sun, no pine trees, no fields will exist!

No white ones, no blue ones—there'll be nothing at all.
And a tyrant will come to ruin and kill.

And women give birth in dark ravines,
And riderless horses will whinny and whirl.

Through white stone foundations grass will grow green.
And gloom, like a mammoth, will sink to the earth.

And maltreated women will weep in the squares.
No white ones, no blue ones—there'll be nothing there!
Not even in dreams nor before one's own eyes—
Nowhere, never be realized. . . .

Bastards,
        you lie!
Cities will rise!

Bright midst hills and valleys
In seven colors will gleam
Not just seven cities,
But seven times seven will be!

Over the universe wide
In golden woods cupped,
I,
Voznesensky,
Will raise them up.

I'm a Kaluzhsky[7] lad,
With a head on my shoulder,

[7] A province in Russia.

In a prickly jersey clad,
With a crackling diploma.
I'm from the same guild here
As the seven master builders.
Storm through the arteries,
You twenty centuries!
I'm a thousand-eyed—

                        with your eyes,

I'm a thousand-handed—

                        with your hands.

In glass and steel I'll realize
All you dreamed of—

                        all you didn't dream.

From my student's desk
I dream, that building elevations
rocketlike

                a hundred-stepped,

soar into world-creation!
And tomorrow night jolting
at 12:45 A.M.
I'll be going

                to Bratsk[8]

to create them!
. . . And watching from the night
Of windows and eyelets
stare at me eyes
from sockets eyeless.

---

[8] The famous Bratsk hydroelectric power station, one of the largest in the world. The subject of an epic poem, "Bratsky GES," by Yevtushenko, part of which I have translated in his *Selected Poems* (Dutton, New York), 1966.

The Triangular Pear

Be a lyrical attack,
It's a crime to retreat!

—A. Voznesensky, 1959

Introduction to *The Triangular Pear*
by Andrey Voznesensky

FROM THE AUTHOR

I am working on a big thematic subject: "About the Discovery of America." It is based on my American impressions. But in the process of work, memories, life, and landscapes of Russia and/or the Baltic burst into the narrative, diverting the author from the main line of his theme.

Other things, quite different, were "discovered." Its heroes now included silver birch trees, sunsets, motorcycles.

The poem drowned like an overloaded ship. But alongside arose an independent organism—"A Poem of Lyrical Digressions." Poems shuffled themselves arbitrarily, outside themes and geography, like thoughts in the head. Their author draws attention to them.

These poems have an independent life and character. Often, sometimes quite independently of the will of the author, they rejected grammar. Sometimes they demanded a fantastic subject. For example, a decapitated head begins to speak. That's going beyond exclamation marks! In other cases the melody demanded to be unfettered, to soar in the heights—it becomes endless like the last note of a singer. Sometimes the barriers of periods and commas interfered with it.

In this collection are included extracts from diaries, newspaper reports. Without them I cannot imagine either myself or my poetry.

THE NIGHT AIRPORT IN NEW YORK[1]

THE FAÇADE

My self-portrait, apostle of the heavenly portals, my neon retort—
New York Airport!

The duraluminum windows vibrate
Exactly like a soul's X ray.

How terrible when heaven is trapped
In your glaze,
Incredible capitals' eroding airways!

Every twenty-four hours
                              you're flooded, like a sluice,
With the starry fates of man-power,
Of dames let loose.

In the bar, your alcoholics are snuffed out, angellike.
By you verbalized!
As castaways
              you reclaim them!
As "Arrivals"
              you proclaim them!

THE LANDING FIELD

They await cavaliers, fortunes, suitcases, surprises. . . .
Five "Caravelles"
                blindingly
                        descend from the skies!

---

[1] Kennedy Airport.

Five night revellers tiredly release their landing gear.
Where has the sixth disappeared?

Clearly it's gone astray—
                              a tramp, a stork, a star! . . .
Cities beneath it
                    like burning dance.

Where is it soaring,
                      groaning, frolicking?
Is that it—
              a fag in the fog that's flickering? . . .

Forecasts it doesn't understand.
The earth below won't let it land.

THE INTERIOR

The forecasts are foul. And, the storm awaiting,
Into the lobby, like partisans, you're retreating.

Governments up there nap in unconcerned pairs.
Chemist-quiet Traffic Control map their routes in the air.

That mighty eye into other worlds peeps.
Window cleaners, like midges, make you weep.

A stellar invader, a crystal monster-creature,
Sweet, yet pitiful, to be a son of the future,
With no wedding-cake stations,
                                  no fools of any sort—
But only poets and airports!

In the aquarium's glass groaned
The heavens,

        welded to the ground.

CONSTRUCTION

The airport—an Embassy accredited
For Ozone and Sunshine!

A hundred generations

        dared not tackle it—
The subjugation

        by single-span constructions.
Instead of stone statues and friezes,
Glassless—

        a glass of blue freezes.

Alongside of swanky booking-offices—
A gaslike

        antimaterial edifice!

That stubborn devil Brooklyn's a crackpot.

The monument of the era's
An airport.

INTRODUCTORY

Discover yourself, America!
Eureka!

Crowning Yemelka,[1]
        I discover, as I delve,
America—in America,
Myself—
     in myself.

I rip off the peel of the planet,
          sweep away dust and decay,
Dive into
    the depths
       of the subject,
As into a Metro subway.

There, pears—are a triangular shape,
          I search in them their naked soul.
The trapezoidal fruit I take
        not just to guzzle and gulp—
But so that the glass of its heart's core
Should light up like an altar!

Get on with it, explore,
       pay no heed at all,
Let them lie that it's emerald,
Your melon is crimson red!

---

[1] Yemelyan Pugachov, leader of a peasant revolt, executed 1775.

Like a hound I snap,
                    like an axe I hack. . . .
Artists hooliganize?
Columbus,
          scan the skies!

The shore winds I find
                    empirically . . .
Seeking
        India,
You'll find
          America!

STILL INTRODUCTORY

I adore
Your flaming floors, soaring to the gates of paradise found!
I am a greyhound,
                   learning the chase at last, I am a greyhound!
I shall overtake you and discern your breed.
Through market depths you speed
                        beatniklike barefooting the ground!

Under the street's fire hydrant my ears spin,
                    like a merry-go-round,
Along gasoline-goaded,
          godless,
               baseballed
                  America!

Coca-colaing. Carillons tolling!
It didn't come that easy at all!

Devilishly teasing, through mansions and backyards you bolt,
At women eyes
          flick to and fro like rifle-bolts!

Your cheap goods from shopwindows were hung round my neck then.
But I searched for the s o u l,
               and forgetting good manners rejected them.
I dived into Broadway, as if in an aqualung dressed.
A flame of blues in a cellar
              came dancing your Negress!
I nearly caught up, but you coolly eluded pursuit.

Read and forgive,
>if in the turmoil I've not understood. . . .

I'm on the roofs, like a gnome, over New York's planning perched.
On my little finger
>your sun glows like a lady-bird.

STRIPTEASE

In the revue
        the dancer undresses, stupidity nude . . .
Do I cry? . . .
Or is it the limelight slashing my eyes?

She strips off her nylons, her bra, her everything.
As from an orange one peels off the skin.

And in her eyes such a longing, like a bird's.
For this dance "striptease" is the word.

A terrible dance. Bar baldheads' whistles, screeches,
Eyes of drunkards swell
               like leeches.
That ginger one, a splattered egg yolk yammers
And clamors, like a pneumatic hammer!
Another's like a bedbug—
             terrible and apoplectic.
The saxophone's cacophonically apocalyptic!

I curse your scale, O Universe,
Your bridging Martian radiance,
I curse,
      adoring, wondering and appealing.
As a woman dances to jazz, unpeeling! . . .

"You're America?" like an idiot I'll ask her.
She'll sit down, grab a gasper.

"Kiddo," she'll say, "you've got the cutest accent!
Order me a Martini and an Absinthe."

DIGRESSION INTO THE SEVENTEENTH CENTURY—
A BALLAD OF BEHEADING

In their Majesty[1] amusement they seek.
Crowds from Kolomna and Klyazma[2] sweated.
"Their mistress—

        a counterspy
        Anglo-Swedish-German-Greek . . ."
To be beheaded!

The Tsar is terrible: jadelike, skinny,
Growing blacker than anthracite.
Over his face his eyes go skidding,
Like a stalled motorbike.

And when her head rolled off the block
Till by his jackboot's toe it stopped,
He raised it up

        over the crowd—
Like a turnip with a red-beet top!

His fingers clutched her cheeks, like claws they grip,
Cracking the bridge of her nose,
Blood from her throat splashes onto his clothes.
He kisses her full on the lips.

The Red Square gasps and sighs,
Then with a quiet groan is stunned:
"A-a-anchen! . . ."[3]
And then to him she replies:

---

[1] The royal plural is used throughout.
[2] Kolomna and Klyazma are Russian towns near Moscow.
[3] German diminutive of Anna (Mons), mistress of Peter the Great.

"My boy mighty royalty
it's not for me to judge your guilt
but why are your hands salty
with sweat

I'm a woman
that is my only guilt
my empire is in my mouth dear
I tremble like a cranberry blood-drop spilt
on your Imperial Royal beard

in these days of construction and fires
what is teeny-weeny love?

you kiss me Empire-sire,
your lips are in my blood

your lavish kisses reek
with borsch and vodka odor.
Epoch how you love me
you I adore
so govern! . . ."

The Tsar froze—with a gloomy frown.
The Tsar gazed with such
                      melancholy-pale
That a foreign guest sat down,
As if bashed to the head like a nail.

DIGRESSION FOR VOICE AND DRUMS— NEGROES SING

We—
>> Homeric drums that throb and thrum,
>>> with martyrs' mournful eyes succumb,
>>>> then smokelike wreathe and rise—

>>>>>> we . . .

You—
>> white as fridges, cold and frigid,
>>> surgical, gauzelike, corpselike . . .

>>>>> you . . .

To you esteemed misters, about what do we croon?

About
your waxlike hands, like white-lime kilns,
O, how their imprints moulded the sorrowful shoulders
>> of our sorrowing wives, O, how they flame with shame—

>>>>>> O—O!

"No! No!"[1]
they thrash us like nags, for tips we cadge,
>> our eyes wax dark, in arenas and bazaars,
but
asleep at nights, our spines shimmer and shine,

>>>>> like windowed stars.

In us
are boxers, gladiators, as in black radiators or in ponds

>>>>>> of carps,

---

[1] In English in the original.

triumphantly, pitifully, reflecting constellations,
    Ursa Major and Mars—
                    within us. . . .

We are Negroes, we are poets,
                  within us spin the planets.
Thus we lie, like sacks, with stars and legends stacked. . . .

When we are kicked about,
The firmament rebels.
Under your jackboots
The Universe yells!

A NEW YORK BIRD

Flying toward me, alights
on the moonlit windowsill
an aluminum bird—alight—
instead of a body
          a fuselage

and on her nut-screwed neck, like a
fairy tongue of flame
from a gigantic lighter
flares
     a woman's
         face!

(Wrapped in a capitalist sheet,
My friend is sleeping sweet.)

Who're you? a cybernetic nightmare?
half-a-spirit? half-a-robot?
a flying saucer there
with the queen of the blues cross-bred?

maybe you're the spirit of America
tired of titillation's ease?
who are you young chimera
with a butt between your teeth?

but they stare without blinking
without wiping off the night cream
those eyes like over Michigan
of another I've seen

she had such puffed-up
gassy pouches under the eyes
bird what do you prophesy?
bird don't lie!

what you know, will you tell me?
something strange outside me
like in a communicating vessel
rises up inside me

the atomic age moans in the bedroom. . . .
(I scream. And, with blasphemic utterance
Like one scalded, my bed-mate
Flops back upon the mattress.)

ANTI-WORLDS: IRONICALLY PHILOSOPHIC

A neighbor we have, Bukashkin by name,
A bookkeeper like blotting paper curled,
But right above him, all aflame,
Like air-filled balloons, float
                          Anti-worlds!

And in them, a demonic-like magician,
Lies Anti-Bukashkin, world leader
And academician, there he pinches
Lollobrigida.

But Anti-Bukashkin's dreams
The color of blotting-paper seem.

Long live those Anti-worlds!
Fantasists—into nonsense whirled.
But without fools there'd be no wise.
No oases without the deserts wide.

No women—
                  only Anti-men given birth.
Anti-machines in the forests roar.
There's the salt of the earth. The filth of the earth.
But without the snake the hawk cannot soar.[1]

How I love those critics of mine.
On the neck of one of them shines,
Fragrant, bald and red,
A radiant Anti-head!

---

[1] Allusion to Maxim Gorky's fable, "The Grass-Snake and the Hawk."

. . . I sleep with windows open wide.
And somewhere whistling meteors probe.
And skyscrapers white
                        like stalactites
Hang from the belly of the globe.

And stuck with a prong into this earth's sphere,
Right beneath me
                        head downwards curled,
Like a lovely little light-hearted moth,
You live,
            my little Anti-world!

Why is it, then, when night times fleet
Anti-worlds each other meet?

Why do they sit around in pairs
And into the TV steadily stare?

They can't even grasp a phrase at a time.
Their first time is their last time.

They sit, forgetting about bon-ton.
But they'll regret it later on!

Look at their ears burning red,
As if butterflies were perching instead. . . .

. . . A lecturer I know yesterday sniped
At me: "Anti-worlds? A lot of tripe!"
I sleep, twisting fitfully at night.
That scientific egghead is probably right. . . .

My cat, like a tuned-in radio set,
Catches the world in his green-eyed net.

FOR THE EVENING

I am exiled into myself
                    I am Mikhailovskoye[1]
my pine trees burn closing their ranks

in my face cloudy as a looking glass
falls the twilight of ptarmigan and elks

nature is in me and in the river
and still somewhere else—outside there

three green groves glasslike quiver
three red suns burn and flare

three women dawn into one another
like dolls within dolls that hide[2]

and one loves me laughingly
another like a bird flutters inside

in a corner the third hemmed in
hides herself like a red-hot ember

she won't forgive me in the least
she will yet revenge herself

her face is shimmering at me
like a ring from the bottom of a well

---

[1] Where Pushkin was exiled by the Tsar.
[2] The Russian toy dolls known as *Matryoshki* have a number of dolls each inside the other.

THE GUITAR

Between paprika and Malaga wines
under fashionable log-cabin skies
like a boat-hauler, bony and stringy
sat a young and predatory singer

a nasturtium fiery-hued
shyly and impudently
the guitar like an artist's nude
lay prone upon his knee

she was gentler and simpler
than the savage at secret rites
and the somber city within her
hummed down to a quiet

or else like the roar in a circus
she madly held her breath,
then—like a motorbike burning
she orbited the wall of death!

we're the children of that guitar
fearless and trembling
among girl friends, the dearest that are
yet as unfaithful as amber

'mid figures of the night
caustically you twist your lips
and to them, like a fuse alight
a cigarette silently creeps

AUTUMN IN SIGULDA[1]

I hang from the platform of the train,
saying goodbye again,

goodbye, my summer,
time to make my tracks,
now in the country echoes the axe,
they're shuttering my cottage with planks,
goodbye and thanks,

my woods their crowns have discarded,
empty are they and sad today,
like bare accordion cases
when the music's been taken away,

we're people,
we're also empty inside,
we too depart,
            thus it is determined,
from walls,
        mothers
               and from womankind,
and that order is eternal,

goodbye, mother,
at the window of your room
you'll stand, transparent as a cocoon,
wearied by the day, no doubt,
so parting, let's sit down,[2]

---

[1] A popular holiday resort and week-end retreat in Latvia.
[2] An ancient Russian custom of sitting briefly in silence after leave-taking.

friends and enemies, be,
proschai[3]
with a whistle you run from me
and I from you,
goodbye,

o, motherland, let's say goodbye,
I'll be a star, a willow over a stream,
I'm no beggar, I won't cry,
thank you, life, for having been,

at the shooting gallery I've tried to make
a 100 out of 10 I shoot,
thank you, that I made a mistake,
but threefold thanks and gratitude,

that in my transparent shoulder
blades enlightenment thrust,
as into a rubber glove moulded
a red masculine fist,

"Andrey Voznesensky"—enough.
If but for a while I could linger
on your sultry cheek—not as a goof,
not as a word—but as "Andryushka,"

thank you, that 'mid autumn leaves,
meeting you asked me something frankly,
with your dog on a dangling leash,
but he strained at it,
thank you,

I came to life again, thank you for autumn's wealth,
that you explained me to myself,
the landlady woke us up at eight,

---

[3] Russian word for "goodbye." The poet uses the English word "goodbye" in the original.

and on holidays hoarsely scraped
that old record, black-market hip,
thank you for it,

but now you are departing, departing,
        as a train departs, you're departing . . .
from my empty pores you're departing,
from each other we're parting, departing,
why's this house now so disheartening?

you're right alongside, and yet very far off,
almost as far as Vladivostók,

I know ourselves we shall repeat
in friends and girl friends, grass blades and spores,
by this and that we'll be replaced—
"nature a vacuum abhors,"

thank you for tree tops that finally blow,
millions in their place will grow,
for your laws—thank you once again,

but a woman flies down the platform paving,
like a fiery leaf after a train . . .

Save her!

DIGRESSIONS IN THE FORM OF BEATNIKS' MONOLOGUES

FIRST MONOLOGUE

I lie, pickled and epochal.
                    Michigan I comprehend
Like in a sponge, time swells
In my freckled cheeks again.

In my face, furry as a bear's den,
                    pupils lie frozen.
I pick out, like trinkets,
Passers-by, sparklets.

With rocket-dromes reverberating,
                    with hovering atomic rain,
The times spat at me.
I spit back at the times again!

Politics? What's the use of agitating!
                    Civilization is suffocating.
Emerald spirit, into you I enter
As with an aqualung into water. . . .

We are beatniks. In the midst of strictures
                    we are wolf cubs, beastlike creatures,
Scandals like shackles
Trail after us clanking.

When, with swollen mummers' mugs,
                    my jazzmen rock,
You thought I was a joke?

                              I—am a judge!
I—am the Last Judgment. Pray, epoch!

My demonism—like dynamite, flashing,
And ripening, will burn you to ashes.

SECOND MONOLOGUE: REVOLT OF THE MACHINE

To E. Nyeizvestny.[1]

Run! Escape!—into yourself, into Haiti, into R. C. churches,
                            into W.C.'s, into Egypt's landscape—
Escape!

We, the ignorant as under Batu Khan,
Work like the machines we man.
In lawcourts their minions insolent,
Swilling glasses of gasoline,
Calculate: who was it in England
Wrecked the machines?
Run! Escape!

Conquering shyness, in the night,
To the one who gave it life
The cybernetic robot cries:

"Give me your wife!
I have a weakness for brunettes," it says, "I love at
30 RPM. So you'd better hand over! . . "

O beastlike belongings of the eras.
On the soul is laid a veto.
We retreat into mountains, into beards,

---
[1] See poem, page 120.

Plunge naked into the water,
But either rivers are drying
Or in the seas the fishes are dying . . .

From women Rolls-Royces are gestating . . .
Radiation! . . .

. . . My spirit, my little beast,
By city side-wings squeezed,
Like a puppy with a broken leash
You rush around and squeal!

But time whistles ecstatically
Over fiery Tennessee,
Like a night-owl enigmatic
With a duraluminum chassis.

[VOZNESENSKY NOTES]

—*and now three nights in a row I've not left Greenwich Village, that picturesque, noisy bohemian quarter of New York. The bearded sphinxes of the Beatniks toss up one riddle after another.*

On a multicolored café hangs a sign: "WHA?" What is "WHA?" "Oh, 'Wha!' is the howl of the contemporary soul" came the reply. Okay, we're listening.

It is dark and puzzling in the basement. Waterpipes hang from the ceiling. Rhythmic prose is being read to the accompaniment of jazz. A sleepy wildman in a torn blouse, like a costume, meets the visitors at the door. His hairy soul steams out of the rents in his blouse. "Wha?" . . .

Pour épater les bourgeoisie? Or fashionable exotics? . . .

My notes can't give a full picture of America. They are like film shots from the car of an elevator, soaring past lighted floors.

Architecture?

I like the Guggenheim Museum—the swan song of Frank Lloyd Wright's genius. Imagine a dazzling, springy spiral, soaring into the sky! Descending the curves of this spiral, on the sloping floor, you inspect the picture gallery. The downward movement is not tiring.

Talents are born in pairs. Arts—are intercommunicating vessels. They exist in twos. This is easy to understand in painting. For example, the naïveté and purity of Zobolotsky[2] is linked to the primitivism of Henri Rousseau, the violent glazed ceramics of Picasso tell more about Lorca than a thousand translations, and the optimistic melody of A. A. Prokofiev[3] is associated with Shishkin[4] and the carved woodwork on the gables of a collective farmers' clubhouse. Something more than mere interest nails me to the hypnotic paintings of Jean Miró. I feel a strange kinship with his disquieting fantasy.

The museum itself is a work of art. The fruity brush strokes of Matisse, the mirages of Klee have finally found a suitable framework. The walls of the museum are slightly concave so that the pictures hang without touching the walls, as if suspended in mid-air. The spiral is a symbol of motion and, if you like, of life.

It's interesting that when the American museum was in the course of construction, I—as a student of the Moscow Architectural Institute—sketched on my drawing board some kind of impossible spirals. My exhibition gallery was conceived on the same principle. And now, looking at that curve spiralling into the sky—even though it wasn't mine, but Frank Lloyd Wright's—I ponder with joy on the unity of human fantasy.

Deafening, dazzling are those American dockyards and markets, overflowing with lobsters and grapefruit, those roads like magnetic tapes, filled with tumult, stridency, music. But sometimes amid all this hustle and bustle one is gripped by something alarming. . . .

---

[2] Nikolai Zobolotsky, a Soviet poet (1903–1958) who spent seven years in a Stalinist concentration camp.

[3] Alexander Prokofiev, a contemporary poet of the right-wing socialist-realist school.

[4] Shishkin, a Russian realistic painter of the nineties.

AN OBLIGATORY DIGRESSION

In America, smelling of camellias,
                 murkiness and ammonia,
In moony hotels, like deers,
               along alleys aluminum,
Puffing like haulage trucks,
Dicks follow my tracks—
(17 brows from the FBI,
Oh my! . . .)

One with a tomato-like mug,
                another, a gallant-like thug,
And their boss—hunchbacked and sick.
Bloodshot eyes like semaphores flick.

Hotels have ears.
          Showers like microphones appear,
And the urinal stares at us,
With the eyes of a plaster goddess.

17 camera shutters clicked.
                17 times through the door crack
Like a house-sprite I bounced,
Through the lens—upside-down!

I survive. Go on talking in hotel rooms.
                Laugh at dirty jokes as well.
17 Voznesenskys doomed
To lie in cassettes, in safes, as in hell.

With gaping grub traps,
             like a forest with pins-and-needles hands,

Prisoners in a game of "Hands Up!"
Frozen stiff my doubles stand.

One frozen with a lobster between his teeth.
                    Another like a chandelier, suspended in a leap.
And that one's hands with water's trickling.
But now for sure he'll never drink it!

17 Voznesenskys hollered,
                    but without a voice. My shout
On a tape recorder rolled,
Like a crimson tongue ripped out!

I'm unwound, I'm thrown around,
                    they drag me off for questioning. . . .
I'm long ago at home. Safe and sound.
But somehow there's no me left in me.

But there, in far-off bombproof hide-outs,
                    in spinach-tinted jackets, spies,
Like radiologists and night owls,
Examine me on film—all eyes.

One grew bloated, mosquito-like.
                    Another croaks: "Did he make it, that Muscovite?!"
The hunchback grows gloomy. He keeps mum.
But his eyes burn crimson.

It's unbearable to be crucified,
                    transparent to each birthmark,
When, like bullets, you are riddled with eyes
From lips to heels stark!

And fingers in hangnails rusty
                    almost shuffle over one's heart.

"Mr. Voznesensky, does it hurt?"
Let me go! Let me go, monster!

Let go, Quasimodo dandy!
                          My spirit burns, bleeding
From the Statue of Liberty's piercing eyes
And the tender stares of the FBI.

A DIGRESSION IN THE FORM OF A MOTOR RACE ON A VERTICAL WALL

To Hon. Master of Sport N. Androsova

Beneath the Big Top, casting a spell,
Around the arena a woman whirls and spins!
High boots—
                    lacquered as a lobster shell.
Lips painted—seductive as sin.
A whizzing horizontal torpedo she pelts,
A chrysanthemum tucked into her belt!

Atomic angel, Amazon!
Cheeks concave crater beds.
A motorcycle buzzes on,
A power saw revving overhead.

She's fed up with living upright.
Ah, crazy cat, daughter of Icarus . . .
Only squares and vestals virginal
Like Roly-Poly[1] stay vertical.

In that orbiting under the tenting,
Between ovations, posters, slights,
The essence of women
                    horizontal
Enters my dreams and flies!

How her orbit circles and flies.
Tears are nailed to the whites of her eyes!

---

[1] A child's toy (wobbly-man) weighted at the bottom, so that however much it is knocked about, it always comes back to a vertical position. See the poem "Roly-Poly" by Yevgeny Yevtushenko in *Selected Poems* (Dutton, New York), 1966.

And over her—a tyrannizing Genghis Khan—
Stands her trainer, Sin-Hi-Chan. . . .

SIN-HI-CHAN: "Isn't she a pain in the neck?
Sticking to the walls like a fly—some trick . . .
And she had a puncture yesterday. . . .
Such intrigues . . . I'll complain
                          to the chief. . . .
And she scratches and kicks like a horsethief."

I burst into her room during the break.
"Teach me," I say,
                  "the horizontal way . . . "

But she doesn't reply that Amazon.
She simply sits and shakes her head.
Inside she still goes whizzing ahead.
And her eyes are full
                  of such sadness
                          horizontal!

AUTO-DIGRESSION

To Jean Paul Sartre

I am a family
in me, like a spectrum, live seven "me's"

seven wild beasts I cannot tolerate
and the bluest of blues

                      seems to flow through a flute!

and in spring
I dream

        that I'm
        the eighth

A DIGRESSION, IN WHICH
ANGLER BOKOV COOKS THE SOUP

Render unto God the things that are God's,
And to Bokov—
                    the things that are Bokov's . . .

He guffaws deafeningly.
Knives burn in the snow.
And like two fire extinguishers
Our red noses glow!

In a sheepskin coat, like a bulldozer
Bokov by a bubbling stream
Stocks up devilish doses
Of fish, fates, sour cream.

Churches, bay leaves, potatoes,
Splash—in the bouillabaisse!
Our galoshes in the snows
Dance like burning brands.

Dances the pot like a Turkoman.
A red ladle flashes the sun.
Bokov's as mad as a Shaman[1]
And mutters:
                    "Ah, charmant!"

(He has bumped off someone, at that!
They say he garotted a cat.
Hunts women till dawning dew,
And spits them on his barbecue.)

---

[1] A witch-doctor, a medicine man from old Siberia.

But I forgive all slandering liars,
When, picking up the balalaika,
The blue-eyed one, like an ikon,
Peers into distant skies

> and lets the *chastushka*[2] fly
> like a golden cloud it soars
> and bears me away like smoke
> to those crimson slippers of yours
> like a conductor's baton stroke
> with playful finger you threaten

"I'll return,

> my little kitten. . . . "[3]

Listen! . . .

---

[2] Folk song.
[3] The first lines of one of Bokov's ten thousand folk songs known as *Chastushki* —limericks sung to a balalaika or an accordion accompaniment.

THE RUBLYOV HIGHWAY[1]

The motor scooters roaring
Past the sanatorium.

Behind handlebars beloveds
Like angels of Rublyov sped.

Frescoes of Annunciation
In white sharply etched
Behind them women shine
Like wings fully stretched!

Their clothes are glistening,
Their wheels are whistling,
Into my shoulders you're piercing
two wide white wings.

Do I fly?
            Do I pass by?
A hawk am I?
A stone am I?

The heavens. Autumn.
Forests crimson.

---

[1] A main highway in Moscow, named after Russia's most famous ikon painter.

STUDENT, MISCHIEVOUS—FIRE AT THE ARCHITECTURAL INSTITUTE

The Architectural Institute's on fire!
Through the halls, the drawings,
Like an amnesty through jail it flies—
Fire! Fire is roaring!

Along the somnolent façade
Mischievously, shamelessly,
Like a gorilla
                    red-assed
It thrusts through a window flamingly!

And we're already graduates
Ready to defend our theses.
In that sealed iron safe
My reprimand's scorching to pieces.

Wounded is Watman[1]
Like a crimson autumn.
Flame my drawing boards,
My city flames and roars.

Like a can of kerosene
Five years and winters fly. . . .
Krasilnikova Kareen,[2]
See how we're on fire!

Farewell, architecture!
Blaze away blueprints,

---

[1] A fine quality drawing paper.
[2] A fellow student.

Local co-ops in rococo,
Little cowsheds with cupids!

O youth, O phoenix, so foolish,
On fire your diplomas and degrees!
Your crimson skirt you flourish,
With your red tongue you tease.

Farewell, period of borders!
Life is ruins and ashes in turn.
We are all flaming and burning.
To live—is to burn.

But tomorrow, in the fingers a-buzz,
Angrier than a bee will thrust
And sting the point of a compass
Out of a handful of dust. . . .

. . . Everything's burned to a cinder.
Exhaled to nix.
Everything's finished?
                          Everything's beginning!
Let's go to the flicks!

[VOZNESENSKY NOTES]

Architecture is a discussion with posterity. The new Kremlin Palace is linked up with the Kremlin towers by its youth, by its contrast, by its sheer downpour of glass and pylons. It is a symbol.

The best tradition is novelty. Mayakovsky and our new poets are nearer to Pushkin than the hundreds who still lisp iambics. Picasso is the continuation of Titian and Rublyov.[3]

---

[3] See page 67.

It seems to me that every artist should be tested by this light-permeated structure as if by an X-ray apparatus.

Pictures? Here you couldn't hang Laktionov[4] and merchant-style, ornamental gilded frames.

Poems? will every poem ring true in these merciless aluminum interiors?

What is important in poetry for me? To look deep into the spirit of man, into oneself, into the interior of consciousness. It isn't a question of form.

Form must be clear, unfathomably exciting, filled with the highest thoughts, like the sky, in which only radar can determine the presence of an airplane.

.   .   .   .

A Settlement in Bratsk.[5] *This settlement of building workers consists of typical little houses made with slag-filled walls. They are built like this: On the left a wall of bricks, on the right plasterboards, and the space between them is filled with slag, with building rubbish. . . . That's how certain poets build their poems: To the left, a wall of initial letters; to the right, rhymes; and between them God knows what is chucked in! And at the same time they forget that which is good for architecture, the qualities of cheapness and standardization, are not at all a plus for poetry.*

---

[4] Alexander Ivan Laktionov (b. 1910), Hon. Worker of Art. Famous painting, *Letter from the Front* (1947), and portraits of leaders. A typical "socialist-realist."

[5] See note on page 30.

THE LILAC "MOSCOW–WARSAW"

To Rasul Gamzatov (A Dagestan Poet)

10.3.1961.

The lilac is taking her leave, the lilac's a lassie on skis!
The lilac's a poodle licking
                                              my cheeks!
The lilac's lamenting,
                            the lilac's a queen.
The lilac's like blazing acetylene!

Sat Rasul Gamzatov a bison somber.
Said Rasul Gamzatov: "Let's take it home."

11.3.1961.

Rasul doesn't sleep. Rasul sweats and curls.
The lilac in the coupé's
                                      a quivering bathing girl.
Oh, how she is sorely distressed and perturbed!
Beneath her are train wheels—
                                              and not black earth.

It's lovelier no doubt to flower in May. . . .
My double, my magic—my lilac, lilac spray,
The lilac like a genius uprears.
She alone can blossom in top gear!

There's one gazelle
                            for a hundred wild goats.
For a hundred tin whistles—but a single flute.

To bloom in the garden—isn't done!
There are hundreds of lilacs.
                              I love but one!

Nocturnal clusters many-petalled drone,
Like an electroplated microphone.

Oh, that tree's a devil!
                              Everyone has migraine.
Like a hundred salutes stands the lilac spray.

12.3.1961.

The customs official shuddered: "What! Living plants?"
The official, groaning, forgot his regulations.
Oh, sense of wonder, that wonderful seventh sense! . . .

Around planets, like an emerald lustre circulating,
Twixt galaxies and villages soars
the whistling tracks
                              of a lilac in flight!
Laughing at the earth, its grass, its laws. . . .
P.S.
I read the letter: "The lilac has died."

P.P.S.
"Oh, hell!"
              I cried.

DIGRESSION ON PRIVATE PROPERTY

Hey there, listen!
         What's up? Tell me! Come closer, so . . .
Atavism? . . .
Or maybe—cancer of the soul?

To the best woman in the world,
         to the very youngest, misfortune came.
And she was such a nice girl
With eyes of Fayume[1] flame.

Motorcycles she commandeered,
         on which she steered and tore,
Like an arrow veers
Into the furious, roaring flanks of a wild boar!

It begins with weekending,
         with limousines, with unshaven husbands hounding,
It begins with surrendering
The purest of her boundaries.

Cars weigh her down without pause,
         bags beneath her eyes, nimbus-like grew.
Someone's mousy paws
Clung like glue.

The autumn garden creeps
         on the powdered bricks.
A human being falls asleep.
         But in the nighttime shrieks!

[1] Fayume, Egypt—famous from time immemorial for its use of make-up to enhance the eyes.

Something's pressing her.

>   And all night—without halts!
The weekend cottage
>   dances
>   on the prisoner
Like on a Tartar dais of skulls![2]

---

[2] It was said that Mamai, the Tartar invader of Russia, feasted on a dais of his enemies' skulls.

GEORGIAN BIRCH TREES[1]

By playful fish streams
by mountains ice-topped
my Russian birch trees[2]
in Georgia rise up

like temple porticos
transparent and straight
in high-columned rows
the birch trees wait

like after long parting
that wood entered I
with arms
                    outspreading
'til nightfall
                    I lie

the twilight's weaving
over me
white
swaying and heaving
trunks slender and light

so straight and bright
in their circular route
they stood

---

[1] The silver birch tree is as typically Russian as an oak is English—but not typical for Georgia.

[2] In the original the poet repeats, "Birch trees in Inguri, Birch trees in Inguri." Inguri is a place in Georgia. The incongruity would be understood by most Russians; but I have altered it to make it understandable to English readers.

          like searchlights
in Moscow
          salutes

I love their weightlessness
their highest of heights
my conscience I test
by their purity white

DIGRESSION IN THE RHYTHM OF ROCK 'N' ROLL

To Andrey Tarkovsky

TRUMPET SCORE

Rock
   'n'
      roll—
            see the sandals kick!
Down
     the drinks—
              face a neon-sign.
Roars the music,
           scandalously rocks,
Prances the trumpet,
             pythoness-like!

Step on the gas—
            dead-ended you go,
Two cars
       crash—
           like it or lump it.
Ace
    of spades—
           a white-dickeyed Negro,
Blow,
    man,
    blow
        that terrible trumpet!

Rush
    to that
         trumpet, like to a funnel,

Faces,
        clobber,
                parakeet shrieks,
Two madonnas
            "à la beatnik,"—
Cram that meat-grinding trumpet!

A ginger
        Negro—
                a sun in eclipse.
A sinister jester
            of kingdom come.
Above the globe,
            an umbrella held by a fish,
Dances
        a parachute with the Bomb!

Beards like torches. Rock 'n' Rollers.
Everything's inverted. Balls for rollers.
Youths in skirts roll 'n' shock,
Women with painted mustaches rock.

(Time, stop still! You're so disgusting! . . .)
Chucked at the wall,
                watches are busting!

"I wore a watch—now it's in pieces!
Barefoot on splinters—Oh, you're a doll! . . ."
Over white lino, rock 'n' roll. . . .

(Look out! Or time will cut you to pieces, Miss!)
        . . . over the white linoleum rocks
Blood, blood—
                in crimson tracks!

BOYS' CHOIR

Mix us crimson cocktails!
Give us Bloody Marys!
Like a boiler beneath our shirt tails
Steams a prehistoric spirit!
We're the by-products of atomic fallouts.
For fathers who gambled and lost—
                              we're the pay-off.
Instead of TVs, empty grates we'll get.
Like funeral wakes our Bacchanalias dread
In cows' bellows and scooters' zoom . . .
Rock!
        Rock!—
                the dance of doom!

THE WHOLE ENSEMBLE

Over this land, so lovely and crystalline,
Cachinnating like a cannibal,
The Mississippi
                Messiah
Mister Rock conducts the carnival!

Wool squeaks beneath his celluloid dickey.
Mister Rock's as pale as an idiot.
Mister Rock has the mug of an escalop.
Mister Rock—minister, prophet, lunatic;
On passers-by
                skyscrapers dance—
Jackboots stamping on the ants!

FOR THE VIOLIN

From the Rockies to the Atlantic,
All neonized from tears,
Our youth is rocking frantic . . .
    ("only not her, Rock, Rock, she's not yet seventeen years! . . .")
Our youth strains like a lunatic . . .
Rock! 'n' Roll! Rock! 'n' Roll!
SOS! SAVE OUR SOULS!

THE LENIN SEQUOIA

In automobiled California,
Where sunshine smells of colophony,
There's a park of sequoias.
                              One of
Them dedicated to Ulyanov.

"A Lenin Sequoia?!"
                        Hail!
Complete confusion, as in hell.
"A Lenin Sequoia?!"
                        Like a thunderclap!
The sheriff, with unbuttoned fly-flap,
Like a poodle with red tongue aflare,
Rushed to audience with the mayor.

"Mr. Mayor, sedition is afoot.
To Moscow stretch its roots. . . .
Ooh! . . ."
The mayor swallowed his cigar. Sound the alarm!
Into the Mississippi
                        he leapt fully armed.
All over America sirens call.
In underground shelters the populace weeps.
Tanks like giant tortoises crawl.
River dredgers arm to the teeth.

            .   .   .   .   .

In the park's center a gaping hole.

Who planted you, sequoia of old?
Who heeded that ancient tree?

The tablet has burned in the furnace.
No sequoia exists.
    A sequoia there is!

    At noon exactly
                 every 24 hours
    over the skyscrapers
    brightly gleams
    the crown of a parachute as it flowers,
    an outstretched searchlight beam
    strikes the great trunk of a tree
    illuminating triumphantly
    no sequoia exists
    a sequoia there is

    just like that,
              over Moscow saluting,
    leaves
        mysteriously
             hanging and guarding,
    each of us has his own Sequoia rooted,
    we cultivate a conscience like a garden.

    the sequoia is my light and my comrade
    no matter in what land my vocation.
    midst emergencies and escapades
    midst carnival yells and ovations
    when it's all unbearable to me

    I sink into a pool of shade
    beneath its silver canopy

    its conversation—needs no translation. . . .
No sequoia exists?
A sequoia there is!

[VOZNESENSKY NOTES]

I Love Lorca

I love Lorca. I love his name—light, flying like a boat, humming like a theater gallery—sensitive as the moonlike disc of a radar, smelling bitter and pungent as orange peel. . . .

Lorca!

He had been a tramp, an actor, a fantaseur and a painter. De Falla said that his musical gifts were no less than his poetic gifts.

I never saw Lorca. I was born too late. I meet with him every day.

When I see two moons of burnished brightness—one in the river, the other in the sky—I want to cry out like one of Lorca's boys: "Midnight, bash the plate!" When they say "Córdoba" I already know it—two misty Córdobas,[1] "the Córdoba of architecture and the Córdoba of waterlilies," merging into one in the evening waters. I know his heart, vulnerable, transparent, "like silk fluttering from rays of light and the delicate sound of little bells." I don't know anything to equal the psychological accuracy of his "Unfaithful Wife." What purity, what pearls of feeling! I love to listen how, in his ballads (quoting Lorca),

> Gypsies and seraphims
> Play on accordions . . .

He was killed by the Francoists on the eighteenth of August, 1936.

The criminals tried to explain that it was an accident. Ah, those "accidents"! . . . Pushkin—a misunderstanding? Lermontov—an accident?!

Poetry always means revolution. The songs of Lorca meant revolution to those hypocritical neo-inquisitorial jailers—for in them,

---

[1] See "Saint Raphael" in *Lorca*, p. 73, The Classic Series (Córdoba).

all is internal freedom, abandon, temperament. A tulip on the background of a concrete blockhouse seems seditious, rebellious.

Marx wrote that poets are in need of great endearment. What talk of endearment can there be when the naked heart of a poet is flayed with barbed wire? When I think of the poet's path to tragedy and ruin, I remember Paul Eluard, poisoned by gas during the First World War. The figure of the suffocating poet is symbolic. How can one sing when one cannot breathe? Hoarsely and angrily the voice of Lorca sounds:

> This is not hell, this is a street.
> This is not death, this is a fruit stall.
> I see limitless worlds
> in the crushed paw of a kitten,
> run over by your shining automobile.[2]

Buoyantly metaphorical was Lorca!

> Like the measured tolling
> > of bells
> Is the heavy tread of bullocks. . . .
> Their spirits were decrepit from birth,
> Filled with contempt for their yokes,
> Remembering only two wings
> Which once beat
> > from their own sides.[3]

---

[2] "New York.—oficina y denuncia," lines 55–60, from *Poeta en Nueva York—Vuelta* (*a la ciudad*), pp. 444–445, Aguilar edition. (Copyright by the Estate of Federico García Lorca. Reprinted by permission of the publisher, New Directions Publishing Corporation, and the estate of the author.)

[3] From "Cuatro baladas amarillas III," lines 1–13 (*Obras Compl.*), Aguilar edition, p. 277. (Copyright by the Estate of Federico García Lorca. Reprinted by permission of the publisher, New Directions Publishing Corporation, and the estate of the author.)

Metaphor is the motor of form. The twentieth century is the century of transformations, of metamorphoses. What is a pine tree today? Perlon? A fiberglass rocket?

My furry celanese jumper has conifer nightmares. It dreams of the rustling pine needles of its hairy-branched ancestors.

Lorca—this is association. In his poems, the night sky "gleams like the croup of a colt."[4] The wind cuts off a head leaning out of the window, like the knife of a guillotine.

Things become related, halloo to each other. As in Picasso's work, for example, in his illustrations to the poems of Eluard: the contours of a woman's face merge into the shape of a dove. Brows blossom into palm leaves. What's this, hair? Or the wings of a dove?

I have also seen the paintings of Lorca and through them, as in his ballads, flows the same grace and delicacy of the Spanish Gypsy.

But in his poetry his pictorial sense bursts all bounds. Lorca loves local color. How piercing is the green of his "Somnambula Ballad"![5]

> Green, how much I want you green.
> Green wind. Green branches.
> The ship upon the sea
> and the horse in the mountain.
> With the shadow on her waist
> she dreams on her balcony,
> green flesh, hair of green,
> and eyes of cold silver.
> Green, how much I want you green.

How delicately and precisely moonlight is depicted as green— "emerald," let's say!

And in the poem "The Murder of Antonito El Camborio," red is the dominant color. And heavy gold floods through "Four Yellow

---

4 From the poem "The Death of Antonito El Camborio."

5 From *The Selected Poems of Federico García Lorca*, translated by Stephen Spender and J. L. Gili. (Copyright 1955 by New Directions. Reprinted by permission of the publisher, New Directions Publishing Corporation.)

Ballads." But the most terrible and powerful gamma of Lorca is black in "Ballad of the Spanish Civil Guard."[6]

> Black are the horses.
> The horseshoes are black
> On the dark capes glisten
> Stains of ink and of wax.

"Black, black," the poem insistently repeats. "Black!" One has a blackout from these gendarmes. Color becomes a symbol.

> But the Guardia Civil
> comes scattering fires
> by which, young and naked
> the imagination is seared.
> Rosa of the Camborios
> sits moaning by her door.
> Her two breasts, cut off
> are lying on a tray.
> And other girls flee
> pursued by their braids,
> through the air in which roses
> of black powder are bursting.[7]

Poetry is, above all, a miracle, the miracle of emotion, the miracle of sound, and the miracle of that "something" without which art is inconceivable. People who lack this inner ear cannot understand Lorca. Oh, the cheerless ears of those eunuchs hanging onto the hem of literature. . . . Poetry has the quality of a magnifying glass, mag-

---

[6] From *The Selected Poems of Federico García Lorca*, translated by A. L. Lloyd. (Copyright 1955 by New Directions. Reprinted by permission of the publisher, New Directions Publishing Corporation.)

[7] From *The Selected Poems of Federico García Lorca*, translated by A. L. Lloyd. (Copyright 1955 by New Directions. Reprinted by permission of the publisher, New Directions Publishing Corporation.)

nifying the emotions of the listener. If there is nothing to magnify,
poetry is powerless!

How can one explain in prose the magic of these lines:

> Let the Señores learn
> that I have died, Mama.
> From the south to the north let fly
> telegrams of blue![8]

I long for Lorca.
I long for his music, with the aroma of slightly bitter lemons.

I want to tell about one other meeting with Lorca.
In Chicago there are 1½ million Poles.

It happened that I was reading there my poem, "The Lilac
Tree" [see page 71], a ballad about a lovelorn little lilac tree that
was leaving its motherland and setting off on a journey.

The room was lit by the lunar-light of the television set. The
sound was switched off. Instead of lamplight there was only the faint
glow of the lilac-tinted screen with its silent floating shadows.

Its light illuminated a feminine figure on a couch. She was a
Pole. She sat with her legs tucked under her. Her people emigrated
to Argentine before the war. She is perturbed and bewildered. Lit up
from the rear by a lilac halo, with bent tremulous shoulders, lilac
hair and gray misty eyes, she herself seemed like a lilac—lost, shim-
mering.

And without realizing it, I found myself reciting about her,
about her fate.

How does she live? What is happening in her soul? At what
straw is she clutching in that empty, alien world?

Instead of replying to my questions she tilted her head, and
began to read, no rather, not to read, but to recite some kind of

---

[8] "Muerto de amor," part 3, lines 21–24, in *Romancero Gitano* (*Obras*
Compl.), p. 378, Aguilar edition. (Copyright by the Estate of Federico García
Lorca. Reprinted by permission of the publisher, New Directions Publishing
Corporation, and the estate of the author.)

poetry. She is transformed. Her voice rings transparent and clear; it is somehow happy and dawnlike.

"That was Lorca," she replied to my astonished look. Her American pronunciation made it sound like Larka.

"A lark?" I repeated, not understanding.

"Yes, yes!" she laughed. "A lark! He is my only joy. I don't know what I would do without him . . . the lark . . . Lorca. . . ."

. . . They killed him on the eighteenth of August, 1936.

The lesson of Lorca is not only in his songs and life. His tragic fate is also a lesson. The murder of art continues. Only in Spain? As I write these notes, maybe the jailers are taking out Siqueiros for his daily exercise.[9]

Twenty-five years ago they killed Lorca.

---

[9] The Communist painter Siqueiros has since been freed from jail. It is alleged he was formerly involved in a plot to murder Trotsky.

Anti-Worlds

MONOLOGUE OF MARILYN MONROE

I am Marilyn, Marilyn.
                          I am a heroine
of suicide and heroin.
For whom are my dahlias blossoming?
With whom are the telephones gossiping?
Whose suede in the wardrobe is squeaking, unwearable?
It's unbearable.

unbearable—not to fall in love,
unbearable without an aspen grove.
unbearable is suicide,
but still more unbearable
                          to be alive!

Sales. Kisses. The Boss neighs like a gelding.
(I remember Marilyn.
In a Drive-In watched by motorcars.
On a cinema-screen of a hundred yards,
in a biblical heaven
                          with a harvest of stars,
on a prairie with billboards above her
Marilyn breathed,
                          and they loved her. . . .

They're exhausting,
                          those motorcars thirsting.
Unbearable),
                unbearable
one's face in seating of dogs' smell reeking.
Unbearable
                when forcible,
when voluntary—still more unbearable!

Unbearable thoughtlessly to live,
more unbearable—deeper to delve.
Where are our plans? They've blown us sky-high,
existence is suicide,

suicide to battle with trash,
suicide to make peace with its cash,
unbearable, when talentless,
when talented, unbearable no less.

we kill ourselves with money,
with careers, with legs tanned like honey,
for actors
        live not with posterity,
but with film directors' iniquity.

we suffocate our loved ones with embraces,
but by the pillows on young faces
imprints are left, like tracks of tires,
unbearable are our cries,

oh, mothers, mothers, why give birth?
For mother knew they'd crush me to dirt,

o film-star icing up,
for us to be alone is impossible,
in the trolleybus,
in the subway,
in the market,
"Look, that's her!" they're gawking,

unbearable, this naked posing
in all the papers, all the posters,
forgetting
        that a heart is in the center,

in you they wrap their fish and chips,
they crumple your eyes,
                              your face they rip
(terrible to remember in the
France Observateur
my photo'd mug so
                              self-opinionated
on the other side of Marilyn dead!)

The producer yells, munching apple pie:
"You're a doll, your brow—a pearl of great price!"
But do you know *what* they smell of—pearls?!
Suicide, girls!

Suicides—hot-rod kids ride,
rushing to drunkenness go suicides,
ministers go pale from photoflashes—
suicides,
          suicides,
the universal Hiroshima crashes,
unbearable my cries,
unbearable waiting till
                              everything bursts,
                                        above all—

it's inexplicably unbearable.
why, hands simply reek of gasoline!

they burn unbearably on the aquamarine
from you—those farewell tangerines. . . .

I'm a weak woman. Shall I ever get things right?
better now—
          outright!

Poets and Airports

MAYAKOVSKY IN PARIS[1]

To the Pavement Artist

Lily Brik on the pavement lies supine,
ironed flat by automobiles.
Like pieces of money pupils shine
under solid soles and rubber heels!

Passers-by chuck down a reward.
And wound-like,
Mayakovsky,
         early, plaintive,
as a picture-framed playing card,
on that bridge is painted!

Poet, with Your love, how're things?!
One would have to play with fate
so that one's image,
         like Hiroshima, clings
imprinted on the pavement flat!

The crowds hurry over Your breast,
the Seine surges under Your spine.
And like a lady-bird, the autobus
crawls over You, comic'ly hurrying by.

What emotion grips You, what nervousness! . . .
The bridge hovers and vibrates.

---

[1] While on a visit to Paris the poet came across the work of a pavement artist on one of the Seine bridges. It was a reproduction of a portrait of Mayakovsky and his love, Lily Brik, from a 1923 edition of his famous love poem, "About This." Hitherto neglected and untranslated, the poem is now included in my volume, *Mayakovsky* (Hill and Wang, New York, and Dobson, London), 1965.

Paris, in its very asphaltness,
the night
      like lilac
          permeates.

A prodigal. A carrot-buttonhole Futurist.[2] A genius
stuck to a bridge. You were Earth's ambassador. . . .
No one came
      to Your exhibition,
            Mayakovsky.[3]
               Heinous!

We would have come, Volodya.

We would have asked You to recite.
Ah, how fatally You are missed!

O lips now sealed
with a leaden stamp at night.
Your spine's not a flute—[4]
It's the aluminum flight of a bridge.

Mayakovsky, You are a bridge.
Over time,
      like a gymnast,
Your boots touch ROSTA's[5] edge
and Your palms
        touch us.

---

[2] As a Futurist in 1914, Mayakovsky sported a carrot in his buttonhole.

[3] None of the leading writers, poets, or politicians came to visit Mayakovsky's *Exhibition of Twenty Years' Work* in Moscow in 1930. A short time later Mayakovsky committed suicide.

[4] Mayakovsky wrote a poem in 1914 called "A Flute of the Spine."

[5] Rosta was the original Tass Agency, i.e., the Soviet Government's official news service, for which Mayakovsky worked during the Civil War, writing and drawing thousands of agit-posters.

Like a bridge is Your square,[6]
under that bridge motorcars must go—
to Mayakovsky underfoot there
Mayakovskian Moscow!
Mayakovsky thunders at scurrility
with Mayakovskian purity.

Thousands of stadiums shout to You:
How're You thinking now?
                              how're You breathing
Comrade Bridge? Mayakovsky anew!

A bridge. Paris. Stars unsheathing.

Lurking below, the sunset hides.
Slashing the firmament's space
the red tracks
                    of a jet plane glides,
like a razor across the face!

---

[6] The former Triumphant Square in Moscow is now renamed Mayakovsky
Square, next to Pushkin Square.

WITH THE BURNING WASPS OF WINDOWS

With the burning wasps of windows
Paris is like a lilac bush.
You disturb and quiver its silver
with frosty villas shivering brush.

With overhanging eyebrows buzzing,
fearful from sorrow and delights,
Paris,
      like a bee,
             I gather
into the bags beneath my eyes.

NIGHT

How many stars up there!
Like microbes
          in the air . . .

LYRICAL RELIGION

Surge enthusiasts
on the sorrows of malthusianism
multiplies Mankind's
                    procession
in lyrical
        progression!

(But Sigulda[1] is all in lilac
as in a broken mirror seen,
green on silver piling,
silver on green.)

In hazel groves, on boats, in fields,
with guilty embarrassment,
its laws are finally revealed
by lyrical progression!

Let the faculty flutter the eyelids
of Euclids and Engelhardts.[2]
$2 = 1 > 3,000,000,000!$ [3]

Romes and Greeces come to perdition.
Professors, for impudent runts,
repeat by heart their progressions,
the way wood-goblins grunt.

You ask: "Is it true by the given data
that the heart at the moment of rendezvous,
can push four loaded freightcars?"
Yes, that's the law! It's true!

---

[1] See poem on page 52.
[2] Author of *A History of Tsarist Censorship*.
[3] Population of the earth.

Dance, my academician!
Guffaw till Monday evening
over the physics of grieving
lyrical progression!

(You're younger than I? Older!
Over lime trees, eyes are brooding . . .
Your science is an age-long
hallooing, cuckooing.)

World revenge menaces
from ripening lilacs pressing—
                who is slapping faces?—
lyrical aggression!

TVARDOVSKY SANG IN NOCTURNAL FLORENCE

Tvardovsky sang in nocturnal Florence,
as they sing in the river forests,
without a trace of falsity
in the countryside of Smolensky,[1]

and the usual haughty-white
mask of his inscrutable face
rolled over the tapestries,
lit up,
      like teardrops traced,

and the porter downstairs, astonished,
recognized in that melody disarming
the curves of Rublyov's[2] Madonnas
and swanlike Modigliani,

he couldn't understand, in a modernistic
mirror reflected, between us soared
the terrible image of
              the Great
Patriotic War,[3]

she alighted, an anxious troubled bird,
and, as into her hollow eye-sockets we stare,
one of us knows without a word,
for the very last time he's singing there.

And suddenly our interpreter silent grew,
as over the Volga they await the ferryman,

---

[1] Smolensk is a large city in western Russia.
[2] See footnote, page 67.
[3] Soviet nomenclature for the Second World War.

and her eyes burn and flare anew,
like fires on Zhiguli's[4] towering banks.

What are you, Irina-Rowan,
singing about?
With the bloody knife of war
your beloved Russia is gouged,

ah, the fate of these women,
enveloped by war, remember,
is by no judge cognizable,
beneath ashes burn red-hot embers.

Is it easy to chat about de Santis,[5]
when through your whole face leaps
a parachutist-commando
                              descending
tugging the ring with her teeth!

Jealous of men who simulate,
over you hangs, like a summons from above,
your first
              Great
Patriotic Love,

for my mistrust forgive me. . . .
But I can't make you out, I cry
when with a gait of whimsy
a señorita
              passes by,

---

[4] In that area, near the Great Volga Hydro-Electric Power Station, the right bank of the Volga rises over 1,000 feet above the river's surface.
[5] Giuseppe De Santis (b. 1917), Italian film director of the neorealist school and a Communist.

beating the villa with stiletto heels,
but in her sunglasses ornate
like water
       in burning
            wells
her pupils scintillate!

Snow Smells of Apples

FIRST ICE

A girl in a phone box is freezing cold,
Retreating into her shivery coat.
Her face in too much make-up's smothered
With grubby tearstains and lipstick smudges.

Into her tender palms she's breathing.
Fingers—ice lumps. In earlobes—earrings.

She goes back home, alone, alone,
Behind her the frozen telephone.

First ice. The very first time.
First ice of a telephone conversation.

On her cheeks tear traces shine—
First ice of human humiliation.

BIKES[1]

To Victor Bokov[2]

The bikes are lying
in the wood in the dew
the road is shining
through birch trees new

they reached there, they fell,
handlebar to handlebar
pedal to pedal
mudguard to mudguard

you'll never stir them—
not on your life!—
those torpid monsters
with chains intertwined

so big and surprised
stare from the earth
at hazy-green skies
resin oozes
          bees purr

amid clamorous plenty
mint and camomile deep
they lie
forgotten
and sleep
        and sleep and sleep

---

[1] There are no capital letters or punctuation in the original.
[2] See poem, page 10.

CROWNS AND ROOTS[1]

They carried him not to entombment.
They carried him out to enthronement.

Browner than bronze,
Greyer than granite,
Smoking like a locomotive,
The artist lived,
                  dishevelled,
To him more divine were shovels
Than sacred ikon lamps!

Languished his lilac tree . . .
Like starfall
               in sweat,
His back so steamed
As in the oven—bread! . . .

His house gapes wide open.
Floors yawning holes.
In the kitchen no one.
In the district—not a soul.

The artists are departing,
As in a cathedral,
                   bareheaded,
To birch trees and oak trees
Through humming green meadows.

Their flight—a victory.
Their departure—a sunrise

---

[1] This poem was first dedicated to Leo Tolstoy, but to everyone it was clearly
to Boris Pasternak.

To plains and planets
From tinselled lies.

Crowns fall from the woods.
But powerfully beneath the land
Twist and turn the roots
Of gnarled and wrinkled hands.

A BALLAD OF WORK

To Y. Yevtushenko

Peter
     the First[1]—
Sweater
       the first. . . .

Not Tsarist (from furs swaddling,
From steam bath's musical coddling),
     But coarse
          and pleasant,
               like a peasant!

From revelry sensuous
Vibrated
     the backbone,
From carpenters' wenches
Axes and jackplanes.

    How oak-helves ply,
    Into arcs pulled!
    How the chips
          fly
    To Paris, Istanbul!

    But he merely grunted
    Sturdy and stubborn,
Gaitered legs tower

---

[1] Peter the Great, Tsar of Russia (1672–1725). Famous for being not only a Tsar but a hard-working shipwright, mechanic, and craftsman. He went to England to work in the shipyards and to learn how ships were built.

Like a turret-crane tower.
But there in The Hague
A peasant and ruffian,
A rank ragamuffin,
With a nose like a tuber—
Peter?!
Rubens?[2]

But maybe, not Peter?
But maybe,
              not Rubens?
He lived amidst metal,
Rubbish and rubies.

Where in awful abysses of rebellions
                              and putsches,
Like barrels
          of cabbages,
                    waddled
                         Capuchins!
He lived so bedraggled, in unbuttoned breeches,
His belly
        shook
              like a shaggy
                         beetroot.

Unshaven,
          already half-mad in his heart,
His ears stick out
                like handles of a mug.
His long hair steaming,
                    as if over a tub.

---

[2] Also Peter.

He thought.
                     All this was but
                                     the start,
The start, giving birth to Saskias[3] and Shebas[4] . . .
Sweat pours—
                     olympic,
                               triumphant,
                                         imperial!

Sweat pours
            (to become the rich gems
                                     of Bathsheba).

Sweat pours
            (to reflect
                       through Versailles
                                         founts and rills[5]).

Sweat pours,
            through the epochs transposing
An artist into a god,
                      a tsar—into a peasant!

That proud moisture over you splatters,
Caressing your brow
                    and stinging like nettles.
You were like gods—slaves to your craft! . . .

In a worker's tunic
I stand ready to start.

---

3 Wife of Rembrandt, subject of his paintings.
4 Queens of Sheba.
5 In the fountains and statues of Tsarskoye Selo, Petrograd.

Recent Poems

OZA

[EXTRACT]

You mighty mass of computered
programmed animals—accursed be!
That I was reputed
a poet of your decadence,
accursed be me!

The world's no junk for an auction sale.
I'm Andrey not an anonymous cipher.
All progress is reactionary
if it means man's downfall.

We can't be bought with cold toys,
nightingales mechanical!
Most important in life is humanity—
Have you beauty? Sadness? Joy?

Land of mine, country of beauty,
land of Rublyov, Blok, Lenin,
where snow astounds with its purity
bewitching and compelling. . . .
Above, there is no predestination—
       to bring
             the world
                  to salvation!

NYEIZVESTNY—REQUIEM

IN TWO PACES WITH AN EPILOGUE

*In memory of Lieutenant E. I. Nyeizvestny[1] of the Soviet Army,
who fell in the attack on the Second Ukrainian Front. Eventually
it turned out that E. Nyeizvestny was alive, and he was awarded
the Order of the Red Star in 1964.*

Lieut. Nyeizvestny Ernst.
All around for a thousand versts
gunfire flattened the heath
with the smoothing iron of death.

The platoon won't advance to attack
but above from the radio antennae
"Attack's the order, f—— you!"
"Right," replied Ernst the Lieutenant.

But your platoon eats dirt,
Nobly immovably prone.
Lieutenant Nyeizvestny Ernst
advances
        to attack
            alone!

Like a snowplow's wings of white
over his tunic quivering
two angels hover—death and life—
double knife blades glistening.

---

[1] In Russian, the name means "unknown," and has overtones, of course, of
the Unknown Soldier.

Cried Death: "You fool, go back!
You're the loneliest man on earth.
Against whom do you attack!
Against a colossus, Ernst!

Against
    a fourmillionfivehundredfortyse-
    venthousandeighthundredtwentythree-
    squarekilometers monster,
against
    20,745,243 muzzles, aimed at you,
    against an army, a fleet
    and a mad rabble,
                against
    kulturträger gangsters,
    against national socialism,
                    against!

Against world bestiality's tide!
Greenhorn, you're already dead! . . ."
"Not yet," Ernst decides,
and takes the
           VERY FIRST STEP!

And Life cries: "Listen, Eric,
life needs living men.
In the garden blooms the lilac
no longer for you—but them,
there won't be
           1945, 1949, 1956, 1963, there won't be
and only the formula for murdered humanity will become
             $31^n \times 6{,}385 + 1$,
and you won't enroll in the university
and won't transfer to sculpture,
and never sense that hot plaster smells like warm milk,

there won't be the studio on Sretenka,
kept shut by a piece of wire,
there won't be the exhibition in the Manége,[2]
and on the 17th of April 1964 Dinka[3] won't come running up
and won't stick her little finger in the plaster,

                                with nail polish peeling off,
and she won't break away, won't run away,
and won't run back again next morning, and again won't run away,
and won't ever come running back again, and won't bring

                              from the Central Market
fresh cherries, wrapped

                in the 'Komsomolka' of April 27th,
and a fiery-red cherry
      won't roll down
                  the plaster pedestal of the
                          Cosmonaut. . . .[4]
There'll be no Dinka, no Cosmonaut
                (or rather, there will be, but not
for you, but for white-faced Mitki Filin,

                        who did not
jump out of the dugout that day),
and for you there will never be anything
no!
no!
no! . . .

Only Mother will collapse by the door
with an envelope in which is death,
you understand, Eric, now?"
"And how," Ernst caught his breath.

But higher than life or death,
a piercing laser beam band

[2] Where Khrushchev made his famous diatribe against modern art. See page xx.
[3] His wife.
[4] A monument to the Soviet cosmonauts, made by Nyeizvestny.

a THIRD demands more than both
that which distinguishes man.

Beasts take away life.
Only humans give.

Like an alarming searchlight
in contrast to any beast,
the quality of self-sacrifice
to humanity is unique.

Russia, too, is unique,
mine, most uniquely,
unique too our thanks,
that you have picked on me.

.   .   .   .   .

Lieutenant Nyeizvestny Ernst,
when by women surrounded,
like a tipsy ichthyosaurus
you sleep at my table soundly,

when Philistines and squares
about your orgies pule
I sense then
                how a monument
tosses and turns inside you.

Politely I bared my head
and to them politely said:
"Of course, you're clean-shaven and neat
and your taste has always been right.
But have you ever been
for your Motherland killed outright?"

Notes

First, the *division of the poems:* I have kept to the poet's own division as far as possible, in chronological order. As he himself says in his notes, he intended to keep the poems to one thematic subject but in the process of work other themes burst in. Nevertheless he wrote poems about these apparently quite unconnected themes and left them where they came. In his first book, *Mosaic,* certain poems foreshadowed his whole development and the poet himself has stressed the importance to him of such poems as "A Parabolic Ballad" and "The Ballad of the Full-Stop." I have, therefore, put them first, together with three others dealing with the same theme, i.e., the role of the artist in society. And make no mistake, he means above all of a Russian artist in a Soviet Society. It is more difficult for an artist there to go straight for his goal or his enemy, as one can now in a democratic society such as ours, so he goes elliptically, parabolically. But at certain historical periods this was true of artists in other stages of society. He cites Gauguin, as Yevtushenko did Verlaine. He talks of Lorca and Sequieros, of Pushkin and Lermontov, of Mayakovsky, but all the time he has in mind, as do his readers, "the winds that whistled through the bullet-ridden heads of our finest poets." Every day new names of poets and writers rise up, "rehabilitated posthumously," in all the republics of the Soviet Union.

RECITAL ON A BUILDING SITE (p. 6)

For an artist to be labeled a Formalist during the Stalin period was fearful, for it might lead to censure, to expulsion from the Union of Soviet Writers, or even to concentration camp and death. Today Voznesensky is still being labeled a Formalist by some, but the effect is not so deadly. For a while it held up publication of his poems, but the time has now passed when such an epithet was dangerous. And, as he recites, even workers on building sites prefer his "formalistic" verse to the "socialist-realistic."

I remember with what bitterness Eisenstein would say to our class in the Higher Institute of Cinema whenever he had solved some particularly knotty problem of composition and form: "Well, you and I, of course, are Formalists."

TO VICTOR BOKOV (p. 10)

A poet who survived seven years in a Stalinist concentration camp in the North, but one whose spirit was never subdued, as his passionate poem "A Siberian Cycle" gives witness. This was one of the first poems that wrote the truth about Stalinism, from first-hand knowledge. Nevertheless Victor Bokov never lost his passionate belief in life. He is an expert in Russian folklore, a collector of folk songs, particularly the *Chastushki,* or limerick songs. Up to ten thousand, I am told, are in his collection! He sings them accompanying himself on the balalaika, and is always the life and soul of the party. He is also a passionate angler, hence the allusion to his big eyes "like a bass's eyes." He is popular with all the poets and has had more poems dedicated to him than probably any other poet except Pasternak.

THE MASTERS (p. 20)

In 1959 Voznesensky was still intending to be an architect, and went off to Bratsk on the River Angara in eastern Siberia with this in mind. Eventually his success as a poet caused him to change his mind, as he says in "Who Are You?"

> *Starlings strive their best to crow.*
> *Architects to be poet-creators!*

The irony of this gigantic hydroelectric power station, a proud achievement of Soviet industrialization, has recently been revealed by the Soviet's up-and-coming new planners—its output cannot be used for another ten years.

THE NIGHT AIRPORT IN NEW YORK (p. 34)

Here the poet has in mind the architecture of the TWA terminal at Kennedy Airport, which he compares with the "wedding-cake stations" of Stalinist Russia. The proposed Palace of the Soviets was indeed called "the giant wedding cake" by Soviet critics, unofficially and off the record of course, in those days!

AN OBLIGATORY DIGRESSION (p. 59)

In this poem the poet uses, for the first time in Soviet literature, the Russian slang name for the Russian Secret Police of the former GPU, now the KGB: *stukachi*, an onomatopoeic word expressing the sound of the footsteps of the police "shadow" always dogging the heels of any suspect. So, as in all his other work, the poet is writing not only about the United States but also about the USSR.

DIGRESSION IN THE RHYTHM OF ROCK 'N' ROLL (p. 77)

Here the poet uses several English words in the original: Rock 'n' Roll, How do you do, Miss, etc., and the final SOS, as well as the English-French menu cliché: à la. I have substituted the Rockies for the Andes for obvious reasons.

THE LENIN SEQUOIA (p. 81)

In this poem two lines stress the Russian letter *S* in capital letters:

U kazhdovo svoya Sequoia
my Sadim Sovyest' Slovno Sad

each of us has his own Sequoia rooted,
we cultivate a conscience like a garden.

The only point I can fathom is an association with the initial letters of the Union of Soviet Socialist Republics, which is in Russian Soyuz Sovyetskikh Sotzialistichikikh Respublik.

ANTI-WORLDS (p. 91)

Amongst the venerable, classic, and museum-like theatres of Moscow there is a young theatre that is the focus of interest for the younger generation. It is known as the Theatre on Taganka (Square). Officially the Moscow Theatre of Drama and Comedy, founded in 1945, it excited no interest until a group of young graduates from the Schukin Studio of the Vakhtangov Theatre joined it, headed by their teacher Yuri Lyubimov, an actor and stage director of that theatre.

They brought with them a production of Bert Brecht's *Good Woman of Sechuan.* It created a sensation by its modern method of staging as compared to the other theatres—in fact it is a return to the stylized theatre of Meyerhold, suppressed during the Stalinist period. This, of course, is new to the younger generation, and as Brecht had not been performed in that period, the whole effect was dynamic. This was followed by Mikhail Lermontov's *A Hero of our Times,* and then by a stage adaptation of Voznesensky's *Anti-Worlds* and John Reed's *Ten Days That Shook the World,* both of which would not have been permitted in Stalin's day.

The productions are reminiscent of a WPA Living Newspaper. There are hardly any settings; it all depends on the actors' presentation of the poems as monologues, or dialogues, in different episodes presented with passion and anger, with ecstasy and mockery, with satire and pain.

LYRICAL RELIGION (p. 101)

In this poem Voznesensky rhymes "Engelhardts" with a mathematical formula, "$2 = 1 > 3,000,000,000$," i.e., three milliards. I have kept the original rhyme.

OZA (p. 119)

About this poem Voznesensky writes:

The poem "Oza" is written in the form of a diary, left behind by someone in a hotel. Oza is the name of its heroine. Its poetic structure is interspersed with prose, embodying that soulless world of the hostile-to-man "programmed beast," a world alien to us.

Since time past evil has often been reflected in art in a phantasmagoric form. I wanted to be in the channel of that tradition. The plot line of the poem is interrupted by monologues of the Physician, the Historian, the Raven, the Poet.

Oza a mythical creation that seems to embody the ideal of humanism, has the association with ozone, and with the Greek word *zoya,* which means life, and also represents the poet's own beloved (it is his wife's actual name).

He curses pseudo-progress, he wants to protect his beloved from Maideneks and Inquisitions. It is a poem about human feeling in the age of the robot and automation. I have had time only to translate one extract from "Oza" which sums up his theme. It is Voznesensky's most complex poem to date.

NYEIZVESTNY (p. 120)

In this later poem, the poet brings in a prose sequence with arithmetical and algebraical formulae. However, I have not been able to discover, to date, what the original formulae refer to!